"How do you retain employees? A cohesive culture, and an environment where employees feel like they truly fit. In *Cohesion Culture*, Dr. Troy teaches leaders how to hold on to top employees, and get the most out of their teams, while avoiding the mistakes that derail so many HR efforts."

**—SYDNEY FINKELSTEIN**, Professor at the Tuck School of Business at Dartmouth College, Author of the Bestseller *Superbosses*, and and Host of TheSydCast Podcast.

"Ultimately, company culture is to blame when an employee leaves—either you hired the wrong person or you didn't support them when they were there. Dr. Troy Hall in *Cohesion Culture* teaches us that in order for organizations to survive and thrive, it is essential that they create company cultures that adopt mindsets of belonging, value, and commitment. When you do this everyone wins: Employees get a relationship that lasts, and employers get the foundation for unstoppable teams."

**—ALDEN MILLS**, Inc. 500 CEO, Entrepreneur, Keynote Speaker, CXO Advisor, Navy SEAL and Author of *Be Unstoppable* and *Unstoppable Teams*

"There are a lot of great books about singular companies and their individual cultures. But there are far too few works that provide a comprehensive overview of building a good company culture. Props to Dr. Troy for putting together an excellent and needed resource. Retention is the new competitive advantage, and *Cohesion Culture* will help you and your company gain that advantage!"

**—WILLIAM VANDERBLOEMEN**, Founder and CEO of Vanderbloemen Search Group and Author of *Culture Wins*

*Cohesion Culture:*

*Proven Principles to*
*Retain Your Top Talent*

by Dr. Troy Hall

ISBN 978-1-63393-929-5

Published by

 köehlerbooks™

210 60th Street
Virginia Beach, VA 23451
800–435–4811
www.koehlerbooks.com

# COHESION CULTURE

PROVEN PRINCIPLES TO

*Retain Your
Top Talent*

# DR. TROY HALL

VIRGINIA BEACH
CAPE CHARLES

# A "Best Places to Work"–
## Tested Leadership Approach to Talent Retention

*Cohesion Culture™: Proven Principles to Retain Your Top Talent* is a bold methodology that challenges leaders to create workspace environments where all employees have a sense of belonging, feel valued, and make a commitment to organizational success.

In six chapters, author Dr. Troy Hall shows readers what a Cohesion Culture looks like, how it sounds, and what actions need to happen to get it right. He explores topics like engagement, authenticity, and mindset to provide clarity to the leadership and employee base relative to coaching, performance, and development.

Each of six chapters begins with a core concept with which readers will become familiar. Introductory chapters provide readers a map of leadership patterns and protocols. In these, to delineate what's expected of leaders before they consider cohesion and retention, Dr. Hall articulates values that encourage cohesion as well as mindsets that embolden leaders to commit to their employees' individual success, which is the key to cohesion. Subsequent chapters center on team dynamics and workplace strategies. Dr. Hall introduces the essentials of what it means to be a learning organization and how learning directs an organization's future success. In the final section, he provides the specifics on how to execute the talent retention model, its global impacts, and how cohesion generates employee retention.

# *Table of Contents*

# *Foreword*

STORIES ARE THE FOUNDATION OF our world. Stories inspire, they help people learn from one generation to another what's important about the culture. Stories are the way we connect, they define how we understand the world we live in and the way we find meaning in that world. My longtime friend, colleague, talent retention expert. Dr. Troy Hall is at heart, a storyteller. He has an ability for taking complex principles and breaking them down into digestible lessons so these concepts are easily understood and adapted.

I've known Dr. Troy for over a decade, and he consistently impresses me with his simultaneous grasp of strategy and creativity. He encourages his clients and participants to be part of the process through active listening and participation even when it comes to a simple task of making a paper airplane. Whether we are at a dinner with our colleagues or at a conference of thousands, I know when I'm with Dr. Troy, I'm going to learn and I'm going to laugh.

Dr. Troy is exceptional at defining real problems, yet more importantly, providing real solutions for companies. His passion for talent retention stems from his exceptional love of people and the leadership lessons he learned from his mom. I have watched him inspire thousands with his message on leadership and creating an environment where people feel a sense of belonging and value. This is the essence of a Cohesion Culture™.

The *Cohesion Culture* book presents over a decade of working within a "Best Places to Work" environment. Dr. Troy shares the best practices of the South Carolina Federal Credit Union living laboratory through real-life examples and practical advice. In his special way, Dr. Troy has presented these proven principles and connected them to *Mary Poppins, The Greatest Showman* and *The Wizard of Oz*.

That's Dr. Troy.

**—MARK SIEVEWRIGHT, FOUNDER & CEO**
**SIEVEWRIGHT AND ASSOCIATES**

*With more than 30 years of financial services experience, Mark advises executive leadership on how to build effective teams and initiate successful strategic business plans.*

*He is a renowned C-suite thought leader who has held senior leadership positions at HSBC Bank USA, Mastercard International, Payment Systems Inc., The TowerGroup, Inc. (as CEO) and Fiserv, Inc. (as President of CU Solutions division).*

*Mark has received global recognition meriting the WOCCU Ambassador Award and was named one of the most influential strategic leaders of the cooperative financial services industry in the last 25 years.*

# *Preface*

SINCE I HAVE BEEN PRIVILEGED to work there, South Carolina Federal Credit Union, under the leadership of CEO Scott Woods, has been recognized seven times by Best Places to Work in South Carolina; three by Best Credit Union to Work For; nationally, by the *CU Journal*; and most recently by Glassdoor's esteemed Best Places to Work. These affirmations provide undeniable evidence that our Cohesion Culture is in place and working.

What is so fulfilling about these wonderful acknowledgments is that we received them not because management said so but because the employees recognized what management did. These three distinct evaluation groups for the state, the country, and the world stage independently surveyed our employee base, and the results were consistent.

The employees at South Carolina Federal feel a sense of belonging, are valued, and commit both to themselves and the organization. This level of commitment shows an understanding that management has aligned values and outcomes between employee development and organizational outcomes with room for everyone's success.

With this book, I make the case that creating Cohesion Cultures in workplaces has a positive impact on performance in all developing stages of a group, and that retaining talent through a culture of belonging, value, and commitment, rather than replacing old talent with new talent, is essential for an organization's survival and growth.

# Behold, The Cohesion Culture

"The strength of the team is each individual member. The strength of each member is the team."

**—Phil Jackson, NBA Championship Coach**

LET'S CONSIDER THIS INTRODUCTION A movie trailer. It is, at the very least, my attempt to offer readers a preview of the coming attractions. Throughout this book, before the credits roll, I show leaders first and foremost the kinds of transformative leadership practices that support the creation of Cohesion Cultures for the purpose of retaining talent and improving performance. As dictated by the situation, a leader plays any number of roles in any given scene on any given day. When it comes to leadership, one is both director and producer. With this in mind, it is paramount leaders recognize that each member of their organization's talent—be it a headliner, a supporting actor, one of a dozen stunt doubles, the makeup artist, or even the caterers—brings value to the whole of the final product in who they are and the role they play—what I like to call a "parts are parts" mentality.

None of the content I share herein is overly complex. It's practical and straightforward. It's a reflection of my contributions along with those of my peers who have led South Carolina Federal to be one of the Best Places to Work. Cohesion Cultures are ones in which employees have a sense they belong, feel valued, and commit to personal and organizational goals. Any involvedness is namely that these three central elements work in tandem. When it comes to HR initiatives in the workspace, a single factor on its own has little impact. Groups must have all three elements—belonging, value, and commitment—to guarantee cohesion. When organizations achieve cohesion, success is a byproduct. Both employees and the company benefit from increased performance, which leads to engagement. Engagement leads to retention of a quality team, which is a core strength of any workplace environment.

## ENGAGEMENT IS NOT ENOUGH

For the most part, *engagement* is misunderstood. Engagement is the outcome of a team working cohesively within a culture of belonging, value, and commitment. It requires more effort than catchy slogans on recruitment posters or using all caps in emails or job descriptions. Somehow, leaders—even me; I'm guilty too—are lulled into thinking that if we repeat the phrase "employment engagement" enough, it happens. Actually, it occurs when leaders support a mindset of cohesion.

Most people relate engagement to commitment when it's demonstrable and affirmed by goal achievements, but that's myopic and misses the mark on the much larger concept of employee and team performance. To consider commitment as a finite path to engagement is shortsighted.

The strength and also the weakness of engagement is that it can be individual. You can have engaged employees without having a Cohesion Culture. An employee can be engaged in providing their individual talents in return for a paycheck, health care and 401k benefits, and educational opportunities the company offers. Engagement can be purchased by incentives such as yearly bonuses, industry recognition, or a company-sponsored vacation. Certainly, these employees can be productive and valuable assets. An employee who gets to work on time, completes tasks, and is self-sufficient isn't necessarily engaged, happy, or satisfied. It simply means he comes to work, does a job, and does not require the involvement of leadership to correct or encourage behavior. To have meaningful engagement, leaders must measure for cohesion and the presence of all three attributes: belonging, value, and commitment. Then and only then can a leader be assured the employee is "engaged" and actually wants to be retained. An employee who is engaged through cohesion feels a strong, often unbreakable community bond with his team and the organization. He understands his individual and collective value. This gives him and his effort meaning and purpose. Finally, he knows his supervisor is committed to his personal development with as much vim and vigor as he is expected to commit.

But what I have found over decades of business leadership, and what I made the subject of my doctoral dissertation, is that individual engagement is not enough to create a truly successful culture of cohesion. What distinguishes a Cohesion Culture is the relational aspects of the talent within the organization and how employees think about and relate to one another. When a Cohesion Culture is in place, individuals are better able to relate to those in other parts of the organization, to those who may report to them, to their colleagues and peers, to their supervisors, and to those in the senior-most positions.

The most obvious result of this is efficiency. Duplicate or unnecessary work is virtually eliminated. Retention is greatly increased, reducing the expenditure of resources on scouting, interviewing, hiring, and training new talent. And all employees are able to access motivation, inspiration, and support from multiple sources—today a manager, tomorrow a coworker or someone from a different department. Unhealthy rivalries, insecurity, and damaging interdepartmental competition become things of the past. Employees now have a big-picture worldview that allows them to see not only how their individual contributions add value but also how every single person's contributions work together to create a transcendent experience: the final product of the moving picture that sweeps us up in such a way that we don't think about each scene but are moved by the story as a whole.

The other result of this is productivity. Through years of research and careful study, theorists have concluded that cohesion is a measurable, attainable phenomenon. In the 2007 *SHRM Research Quarterly*, in her study, "Leveraging Employee Engagement for Competitive Advantage," Nancy R. Lockwood found that employees with the highest level of commitment perform 20 percent better and are 87 percent less likely to leave the organization, which indicates that engagement is linked to organizational performance.

However, it is costly for an organization to constantly be "buying" engagement. To sustain the type of engagement leaders want and expect, companies should instead focus on creating an environment built upon cohesion. This is pure gold for organizations because the research already indicates a vast majority of "engaged" individuals will stay. Through cohesion, leaders have the type of "engaged" employee that will contribute to the overall health of the culture and commit to desired organizational outcomes. And leaders can do so without adding costly programs and monetary rewards that do not produce sustainable levels of engagement. To assure that individuals do not have to be bought every day, leaders should focus strategies and practices toward the intrinsic motivators surrounding the concepts of belonging, purposeful value, and commitment.

So, before going any further, before we begin to think about scouting locations, casting calls, or set design, I want to be clear: cohesion is a causal phenomenon that leads to performance. It is not correlational; it is pivotal. This is an important distinction to explain why successful organizations create cultures of cohesion and why all organizations deserve cultures of cohesion. If you take away nothing else from this book, be convinced that your goal should be the total investment in your business of every single employee, motivated by the Cohesion Culture I will show you how to create. Only then will you have the work of art that is greater than the sum of its parts.

SPOILER ALERT: My dissertation supported the hypothesis that cohesion positively impacts performance in all developing stages of a group. The three elements of cohesion, when measured simultaneously, play a part in producing quantifiable results as cohesion directly impacts performance. Thus, if cohesion leads to performance and performance gives way to engagement, with a measured level of reliability it's true that "cohesion brings about engagement," and for organizational leaders, cut, that's a wrap. Being able to put a valuation on cohesion is principal to leaders who care less about touchy-feely results and more about tangible outcomes. With cohesion, there is an opportunity to quantify the return on investment that cannot be accomplished without all three elements of belonging, value, and commitment.

## MANAGING STAR TALENT

It's impossible to buy a ticket to the Cohesion Culture show without addressing leader mindset. Fundamentally, what leaders absorb influences how they think and ultimately act. A leader's mindset shapes character, specific actions, and thought process. Because leaders expect employees to be engaged and productive, they set goals and expectations to monitor achievement. This in alignment with well-established "people" strategies, and how closely these structures are compatible, determines the level of success a leader will have in creating a Cohesion Culture.

Similar to how moviemakers want actors who are invested in their roles, organizational leaders want employees who fully commit. In playing the blonde bombshell in *A Week with Marilyn Monroe*, to master Marilyn's wiggle, Michelle Williams tied a belt around her knees. Jamie Foxx shed thirty pounds to play Ray Charles, and Renee Zellweger gained thirty for *Bridget Jones's Diary*. Jim Carrey, who played Andy Kaufmann in the *Man on the Moon*, stayed in character even outside filming. In these instances, engagement is a function of performance. Suffice it to say, leaders who commit and model behaviors that convey a mindset of commitment to the employee more naturally lead employees to make a full commitment, ultimately producing that Academy Award–winning performance necessary for a Best Picture nod.

And yet, many leaders don't understand what leads to this kind of employee commitment. Instead, they focus solely on employee task completion—often mislabeled as engagement—and the relationship becomes one-sided. No doubt measuring employee satisfaction with accuracy is challenging. When studies are performed, however, an employee's level of engagement fails to have a direct relationship to performance, attendance, or job commitment. When people are content, they express actions of engagement, but it doesn't prove they have a level of engagement consistent with a cohesive mindset.

As it stands, 63 percent of employees are actively seeking new positions. For well over a decade, fueled by the media, business leaders have identified a war for talent. If anything, the war for talent is really a battle for retention. Organizations spend an inordinate amount of resources in the acquisition phase yet fail to invest resources that develop the stars they already have.

Gone are the days when headhunters could dangle carrots before the darlings of an industry to secure their allegiance, and this isn't necessarily a bad thing. Today's challenge is to hire with a goal to bolt and lock the ever-revolving hiring door without having to promise free refills on popcorn and cola drinks.

Leaders should be more concerned with how quickly employees exit the movie theatre than how many are standing on the red carpet that ushers new recruits through the front doors. Replacing existing talent is costly.

According to Bersin by Deloitte, a digital helpmate to HR professionals, the average cost of a new hire is just shy of $4,000. This includes, at minimum, advertising and background checks, the interview process itself, and the administrative time, effort, and paperwork. When it comes to the cost of replacing a team member, a general rule of thumb is to stretch 25 percent of the outgoing employee's salary across the time it takes to hire someone new and bring him up to the performance standards of whoever he's replacing. Compound this with a recent study that reports 64 percent of today's newly acquired workforce would rather give up a six-figure salary for one that pays less as long as they love the job. Employees want a relationship that lasts, so why aren't employers measuring up?

Well, from an employer's perspective, retaining talent may seem like a chore, like holding the hand of an unruly toddler or trying to impress a hopeless romantic, and if an employee quits six months after he's hired, it's all been wasted effort. What leaders don't often realize is that whether an employee quits or is let go, ultimately company culture is to blame, either by hiring the wrong person into its environment or by not supporting him once he's there.

Take your average feel-good, happily-ever-after rom-com, for example. In the first scene, two people nearly, almost fall in love. Through a series of mishaps or misfortunes, it looks as if one or the other might choose a different path. Then, after rising action, falling action, and the montage—and there's almost always a montage—before the dénouement (which is a fancy way to say the finale), one or both come to their senses or the stars align, because, as we all know, love conquers all. Kismet is met with a desire to commit.

Now imagine if the director shouted, "That's a wrap!" midway through the first scene. Crazy, right? Imagine the unwanted aftereffect if Cary Grant had stood Deborah Kerr up at the top of the Empire State Building or Han Solo had remained frozen in carbonite and was never reunited with Chewie and Princess Leia. But this is exactly the place where a lot of companies stop directing when it comes to their employees. Sometimes this "cut" happens even before an employee is onboarded.

Talent acquisition is something a lot of leaders get wrong. While I'll concede that leaders should acquire "star" talent, it's paramount they direct every employee as if she already *is* star talent. Organizationally speaking, objects of affection don't commit based on the initial romance or the inevitable onboarding. It's nearly impossible to make it seem as if your love is true if you stop putting forth effort as soon as the object of your affection returns it. Beyond being smitten, the relationship is about continuing the romance. It's about listening and teaching; it's about date nights; it's about shared values; it's about believing in one another's narrative whether or not, at the end of the day, they end up together. We strive for long-term love regardless of what the outcome will be.

Employees do not quit jobs; they leave supervisors. The evidence is before us. In its fourth year of collecting data, the 2019 Businessolver State of Workplace Empathy Study cited 93 percent of employees leave organizations because they do not connect with their immediate supervisor. It's not about the money. It is about the culture and how leadership interacts with employees within the culture. If the employee does not feel valued, or part of a team, then they begin looking elsewhere for it. When supervisors fail to support a cohesive mindset and build a culture where employees love to come to work, the romance is off.

## THE EVERYDAY ROMANCE OF HR

This is where HR comes in. Well-considered HR tactics are the everyday romance offerings present in a Cohesion Culture. Somewhere along the way, however, acquisition has become the primary focus of most HR departments. In today's ultracompetitive hiring landscapes, more money and resources are poured into attracting new talent than in keeping their home fires burning. Organizations all too often leave the long-term relationships they already have to chance. Rather than wholeheartedly committing, it's sort of like they sign up for a string of short-term affairs. This is unfortunate.

To distinguish themselves from other employers and woo talent, organizations advertise all kinds of employee perks, everything from flextime to Ping-Pong tables. They want potential employees to fall in love with the job perks. These types of organizations place more value on "buying" engagement than building a work environment where employees are intrinsically satisfied. But if there is no foundation for Cohesion Culture, these benefits are only distractions. What your company stands for matters more than craft-beer happy hours or bring-your-pet-to-work Fridays.

We like to say it's what's on the inside that counts. Don't get me wrong, it's only natural to want to use a wide-angle lens to show off the organization as if every day is bright and shiny. There's a natural tendency to Photoshop bumps and wrinkles, making the organization look younger, smarter, and more appealing. There's an equally compelling narrative as to what makes an epic love story and what it takes to get someone to stick around for the long haul. But you can't buy love, and if that's what your organization has done in the past, it isn't what's retained talent. At best, without shared values, vision, and commitment, what you have is a loose collection of parts.

Employees often need time to know whether an organization and what it offers is right for them. The start of every romance, and this certainly holds true for a culture of cohesion, begins when two people feel as if they're made for each other. This work-relationship lollapalooza is known as a "sense of belonging."

A Cohesion Culture is the perfect setting to foster belonging, as it speaks to employees' primary desires: to be wanted and needed, to find and experience value, and to work committedly toward being successful and accomplished. There's a benefit for management too. They enjoy the lasting, long-term effects of a cohesive relationship where employees want to be part of its culture. So, while you can't buy love—or true happiness, for that matter—in this context, organizational leaders are able to create a culture where employees love what they do, how they do it, and those with whom they work.

HR strategies and practices that move beyond talent acquisition, compensation, benefits, and the onboarding experience ensure the work an individual does is purposeful. Employees must also believe they are being fairly compensated, and that the organization has focused on their wellbeing by offering a mix of programs to fully compensate them in nonmaterial terms as well. Just as a film relies on the structure of context and subplot, securing and fostering robust HR strategies contribute to the success of the organization's overall "story." Just as actors require a script to guide and hone their talents, "people" practices—all those programs an HR department offers— form a primary foundation for Cohesion Cultures to thrive.

These human resource strategies and practices and the Cohesion Cultures that can be built on top of them are distinct aspects of a successful organization; one cannot exist without the other. Real value is created when HR and a company Cohesion Culture are mutually inclusive. Think of it like cameras and actors. On its own, a recording device doesn't make a film. Cameras are only half of the equation, albeit an essential half: they simply capture what actors do in front of the lens. Therefore, it's important to keep in mind that culture exists with or without HR systems; it just may not be a supportive or effective culture in which anything lasting is created. A Cohesion Culture's fulcrum depends on an effective HR department to champion measurable, fully aligned initiatives of employee inclusion, employee purpose, and the assurance that each employee's voice matters.

Additionally, employees must have a performance process that allows for their continuous development and coaching that evaluates what they're doing and why what they're doing matters to other team members and other parts of the organization. This process builds team performance and offers ways to sustain the culture's healthy existence. In and of itself, employee development and empowerment within a Cohesion Culture leads employees to growth opportunities and maturity—first for themselves and then for the organization. When employees feel as if they belong and that what they do matters, we get a glimpse of commitment. Therein lies retention.

Within Cohesion Cultures, commitment is the final act of a three-act play. This is where the fat lady sings and keeps on singing. In the book, Act I is all about leadership and how a leader invests in the dreams and aspirations of her employees and their development; this is what it takes for employees to know they're invited to belong. Act II creates the culture that will retain employees. It moves the conversation forward to align employee goals with desired organizational outcomes. Act III brings the *talent retention model* to life and illustrates how cohesion generates talent retention. When this "tale of cohesion" goes well, it's a storybook ending for the employee and the organization.

# Act 1:
# Be the Leader

# CHAPTER 1

# How We Inspire Others to Do Great Things

"A boss has the title; a leader has the people."

—Simon Sinek, *NY Times* best-selling author,
   motivational speaker, and organizational consultant

**KEY CONCEPTS:**

1.1   *Leader:* A leader is someone who motivates, influences, and enables other to do something they otherwise couldn't do on their own.

1.2   *Leadership attributes:* Seven distinct attributes a leader exhibits to foster a culture of cohesion.

1.3   *Mindset:* To lead a Cohesion Culture, leaders must be aware of how they react, engage, and measure market influences, business opportunities, and complacency.

1.4   *Influence thinking:* This skill combines thoughts and mindset with outside counsel to produce a result.

1.5   *Transformative principles:* Such mindfulness is to embrace and celebrate the leader's potential for change.

As you read through Chapters 1 and 2, keep in mind that there are three important concepts that successful leaders of Cohesion Cultures overlay and integrate into all of their daily actions. First, the leader must adopt the *seven attributes of an effective leader*, understand how *influence thinking* impacts his behaviors, and practice *transformative principles*. Once the leader commits and follows this practical leadership advice, he is ready to begin shaping a culture of cohesion with the sole purpose of retaining talent and helping employees become their best selves.

In spite of the extraordinary advances in the last hundred years, the way leaders lead continues to matter. While collectively we are now able to engage and influence one another differently and on grander scales and on countless platforms, what it means to treat one another with respect and reverence hasn't changed, and how to be our own good stewards hasn't changed either.

We see this again and again in the classic examples of American leadership: our presidents. Historian David McCullough, who won a Pulitzer Prize for his biography *Truman*, shared in a 2008 *Harvard Business Review* interview that

> Truman was no great charmer, but he was admirable and effective in many ways. He understood human nature. He had great common sense, and one of the lessons of history is that common sense isn't common. He wasn't afraid to have people around him who were more accomplished than he. . . . [He] surrounded himself with people who were better educated, taller, handsomer, more cultivated, and accustomed to high-powered company, but that didn't bother him. He knew who he was. He was grounded, as the Quakers would say.

McCullough quoted Truman as saying:

> "Look after your men" means take care of your employees. Take a genuine interest in them. Be empathetic. Treat them well. I'm appalled when I'm taken to see a factory and it's clear that the people running it have seldom if ever walked among the men and women who work there.

Another US president whose leadership I admire is Ronald Reagan. His decisive leadership drew from his strong communication skills and relational abilities. He did what he said; no one ever had to read between the lines. He was one to admit mistakes, and he never took himself too seriously. Soviet leader Mikhail Gorbachev described him thusly: "While adhering to his convictions, Reagan was not dogmatic; he was looking for negotiation and compromise."

While I suspect it came naturally to him, Reagan mastered what is known as emotional intelligence (EQ), which, as I define it, is the capacity to be aware of, control, and express one's emotions, and to handle interpersonal relationships judiciously and empathetically.

EQ dates back to a 1964 paper authored by Michael Beldoch, but the construct was made popular by a 1995 book, *Emotional Intelligence: Why It Can Matter More than IQ.* In it, author Daniel Goleman suggests that emotional intelligence is what separates good leaders from great ones. In a later book titled *Working with Emotional Intelligence,* Goleman offers a solid example of how Reagan's stellar emotional intelligence conclusively swayed how Americans voted in the 1984 presidential election and how EQ trumps IQ.

During his presidency Ronald Reagan was known as "the Great Communicator." A professional actor, the emotional power of Reagan's charisma was shown in a study of how his facial expressions affected those of his listeners during an election debate with his opponent, Walter Mondale. When Reagan smiled, people who watched him—even on videotape—tended to smile too; when he frowned, so did viewers.

Think about this. As leaders, if those we lead don't mirror or model our behavior, at the very least they are guided in their reaction and their engagement. At its core, EQ is an ability to be aware of one's emotions and those of others. Much of the power to inspire others to accomplish great things comes down to compassion and responsiveness. This approach suspends judgment. Instead, it focuses on behavior. How a leader walks into the office first thing in the morning has the potential to set the mood for the rest of the day—as does whether she walks *among* those she leads. There are no ivory towers in a Cohesion Culture.

In a January 25, 2019, article in *Forbes*, "The Top Four Choices of Emotionally Intelligent Leaders," Chris Pearse wrote, "Emotionally intelligent leaders tend to speak less and listen more . . . or as Lao Tzu put it: 'A leader is best when people barely know he exists, when his work is done, his aim fulfilled, they will say: we did it ourselves.'" EQ breeds trust, and when leaders trust their employees, they build openness and credibility.

Currently there's no validated test or scale for emotional intelligence as there is for general intelligence, but keep in mind that EQ can be honed. Some of us, like the Gipper, may have been born with a high EQ, but all of us have the ability to walk a mile in someone else's shoes. In a seminal 2004 *Harvard Business Review* article entitled "What Makes a Leader," Goleman studied 188 companies. His conclusion: "[The] higher up one climbs in the corporate world, the more important emotional intelligence is to effective leadership."

Beyond having a knack at EQ, my mother—known to family and close friends as Fanny—one of the greatest leaders of the twenty-first century, had a superhuman ability to consider other people's perspectives and experiences. She taught me how to "excel at patience," especially when it came to anyone who was different from me. She taught me never to dismiss anyone. She always said, "If you wait, they'll show you." As Harper Lee declared in *To Kill a Mockingbird*, "You never really know a man until you understand things from his point of view, until you climb into his skin and walk around in it."

Of the lessons my mother taught me, I remember two most vividly:

1. If you speak words of affirmation, you will never have to worry about being misquoted.
2. If you have to tear someone else down to build yourself up, you aren't that good to begin with.

Good leadership involves transparency. Although I have made considerable strides in leadership, there were times when I failed miserably at following the advice of my trusted counsel.

In one of my not-so-shining moments when I failed to live up to my mother's advice, my son announced over breakfast that his ideal car was a souped-up Camaro. He described it in detail. I was driven—pun intended—to quash his dream. It wasn't until Vickie, my high school sweetheart and wife of forty-plus years, spoke to me later that afternoon that I realized what I had done. She too pointed out the obvious, but first she asked, "What happened?" Proudly, I told her how I had set the record straight. Next, she asked, "How many more years will it be before he drives?" I answered, "He's twelve, so maybe three and a half, maybe four years." Her response: "Exactly."

My son's proposition was absurdly unrealistic, and I became so consumed with pointing out the obvious that I failed to participate in what might very well have been his first aspirational vision that was bigger than himself. Even now, as I write this, I could kick myself.

When leaders respond in ways that fail to serve others, they miss the point. As my son's leader, in moments where he spit-balls an aspiration, my job isn't to judge or be dismissive; it's to listen. It's a little like when small kids scrape their knees. It's best that the caregiver on hand remains calm. It helps a child figure out how to react, how to take it all in and move forward. How leaders cope directly affects those they lead.

## VALUES THAT ENCOURAGE COHESION

Simple things are sometimes the hardest to see, and there are those among us who, with swanlike finesse, bring light—even life—to dense, distant, and complex concepts. So, even though the swan is paddling madly, her body moves smoothly across the water.

When we're thrust into leadership roles, especially when we're young, we're often consumed with a self-imposed pressure to render decisions with perfect outcomes. We find ourselves in the position to be know-it-alls. But instead, what if you focused on being the Mr., Mrs., or Ms. Learn-It-All?

As we wade further into what it means to be a leader who has the ability to inspire her employees, we see that objectivity, evenhandedness, and letting go of arrogance is the best way to serve others. That said, before leaders focus on the bigger picture of serving others, they must first know themselves. They must become increasingly self-aware. They should know their trigger points, what they believe in, and how they want to act. Only in acting in a way that is true to their individuality will they tap into the entirety of their strength as leaders.

In accomplishing this for myself, a Southern Baptist out of West Virginia, the Beatitudes have been significant. From the Sermon on the Mount in the Gospel of Matthew, Jesus's proverb-like proclamations have guided my effort in expressing what I value in leadership. The following seven attributes inspire us to be the sort of leaders who can rally others to succeed.

1.  **Being teachable.** Being teachable allows us to be open and consider others' input—especially when the idea is contrary to our inherent ideology. When something is new, when it's a perspective you're not familiar with, do you remain teachable? Far from being weak or inconsistent, being teachable enables us to have influence. When we navigate our world with a

belief system that says, "New information is important to me," we model openness and confidence that inspires this quality in others.

2. **Having compassion.** To have compassion is to show kindness. Compassion is the way we relate to one another. It proves emotional connection and emotional intelligence. It enables individuals and groups to have the confidence to strive forward without being hampered by the concept of flawless precision or the fear of making mistakes.

3. **Extending grace.** Grace is the free and undeserved help we give others. Through this process, we regenerate and inspire virtuous impulses to impart strength of body, mind, and soul. Those we lead do not have to do anything or fulfill a requirement, as in a quid pro quo scenario, in order for us to offer grace. Instead, we think of how to serve those we lead as if they are the only ones who matter. As we operate with and through grace, there is an expression of gratefulness on our part.

4. **Seeking truth.** Leaders must also seek truth. When we operate from a perspective that's grounded in fact, not opinion, we are better equipped to navigate conflict. Conflict typically stems from opinion; resolutions stem from truth. Jack Welch, renowned past CEO of General Electric, declared it a leadership hallmark when he said, "Face reality as it is . . . not as you wish it to be." Seeking truth means a leader faces reality, be it opportunity or within an organization's culture. At its core, seeking truth requires a high level of accountability.

5. **Showing humility.** Humility should dictate how we interact with others. When we operate from a position of humility, we show respect for others and take their viewpoints, feelings, and contributions into consideration. This alone establishes value. Such a leader doesn't take credit for ideas that aren't hers. Such a leader shows a brand of kindness that's more reflective of compassion than modesty. Such a leader demonstrates that he thinks about and respects others.

6. **Exhibiting a pure heart.** This may sound too esoteric for the business world, but I interpret being pure in heart to mean having a pure intention. Am I genuine? Am I authentic? There is a gulf between a leader who operates authentically and one who operates synthetically. We shouldn't ask how an employee is doing if we don't intend to truly listen and potentially act on whatever information is offered. We don't say only what we think others want to hear, and we don't necessarily do what others want us to do. We say and do what's appropriate and whatever will produce the result a situation demands.

7. **Bringing peace.** Lastly, leaders are peacemakers. We create a harmonious space in which everyone gets along. We do this by bringing two opposing forces into a space that neither force previously occupied. We create compromise that is consistent and that everyone agrees to. When individual leaders polarize their followers, peace within the culture or within the group is almost always unachievable, and peace must exist. Peace eliminates dysfunction and unrest and is what establishes and solidifies cohesion so, rather than choosing sides within an organization, all sides work together.

While each aforementioned attribute on its own contributes to effective leadership, it isn't until they are steadily and routinely interwoven that we create a Cohesion Culture. Like so much we will discuss in this book, the combined merit of these attributes is greater than the sum of their individual parts. Keep in mind that these values are dynamic, and there is no linear format to follow, no chronological list that can be checked off as if once all seven values have been acknowledged, a leader's work is done.

> ## "You don't have to know everything, you just need to be teachable."
> **—Dr. Troy Hall**

I started with the attribute of teachability because it showcases the impact of the leader's mindset. When leaders are teachable, they are willing to explore integration of the remaining six attributes. In examining your adherence to being teachable, consider the following:

1. Are you a leader that seeks out new information before you find yourself in a position of "needing to know"?
2. How frequently do you engage with peers or subordinates to find out what they know?
3. What are the ways in which you integrate what you have learned into your everyday practices?
4. How do you use information to build upon your value system in a way that eventually supports and sustains your belief system?
5. Do you regularly stop and observe?
6. How much time do you devote to just thinking about a topic or issue before rendering an opinion or solution?

Teachable leaders have a willingness to discover and grow, and the very nature of these seven attributes is to constantly evolve to support the living, growing Cohesion Culture made up of living, growing human beings.

## WHY INFLUENCE THINKING IS IMPORTANT

Influence thinking is the practice of filling our minds with thoughts that are good and constructive, potentially bouncing these thoughts and ideas off a trusted group of advisors, and then taking action. If we have negative thoughts, what comes out in our actions and words likely won't be constructive. This is why we must examine our mindset with the help of others and make corrections as needed.

Influence thinking requires leaders to have a mindset rooted in common purpose, values, and goals. Leaders who practice and demonstrate influence thinking seek to listen to the voices of others, keeping in mind that a voice may be that of a stakeholder or that of a wise counselor the leader trusts as a "grounding board." I like to use the term *grounding board* instead of *sounding board*. A grounding board partakes in a collaborative conversation and offers advice based on fact, not opinion. These grounded individuals are not trying to impress the leader. Instead, they seek a resolution that is best for all. In contrast, a sounding board only repeats what the leader has said, or what he thinks the leader wants to hear. These individuals are commonly referred to as "yes" people.

Influence thinking motivates, influences, and enables others to accomplish their goals, dreams, and aspirations. When leaders practice this mode of thinking, they constantly gain insight from others. Knowing how others see problems and even potential solutions improves the innovation process and the outcomes derived from incorporating a blend of views into the final solution. Being aware of and seeking the voices of others allows for collaborative solutions or results to occur.

Influence thinking allows leaders to build effective teams that operate cohesively to create positive achievement and performance and consistency of thought and action. This is not to be confused with groupthink, in which a misguided desire for agreement results in the suppression of differing voices and perspectives. According to Irving Janis, a research psychologist famous for the theory of groupthink, highly developed teams are more likely to exhibit a particular amount of dysfunction. Unlike the concept of influence thinking, groupthink suggests team members are not fully vested and rarely challenge the status quo or ask probing questions to stimulate critical thought and discourse.

So, we see that influence thinking combines a leader's mindset with outside counsel and results in a leader's action. Action is an essential result of influence thinking. Words without action are much like faith without works. Both are necessary in order for individuals or groups to be effective. Those engaged in influence thinking model behaviors that support and reflect the seven characteristics of an effective leader. Refresh yourself on these characteristics before you move on to the next section.

## A PRESENT MINDSET

Mindset is extremely important in how leaders direct those who follow. The optimal mindset allows leaders to mentor employees rather than judge them; more importantly, it allows leaders to think and respond in different ways. By tapping into this mindset, leaders tap into their organization's collective genius and are better able to navigate their own biases.

As leaders breathe life into ideas, visions, and processes, followers begin to understand the expectations, opportunities, challenges, and consequences of performance and nonperformance. People want leadership that is decisive, consistent, and considerate of how others will feel about any potential decision. Instead of lukewarm, choose hot or cold. Either be the leader with confidence or get out of the way. As the keeper of the chalice from one of my favorite Indiana

Jones movies says, "Choose wisely." It is a cautionary reminder that every leader, intentionally or not, chooses a state of being, whether it's to be accepting of others or closed minded.

How we as leaders think is important, because the condition of our mind directly influences the actions we take. How does this happen? Our core values or guiding principles are formed from how we feel about our experiences and not from the events themselves. These values become the basis of our beliefs.

No leader should dogmatically cling to one particular mindset. Mindset is how each of us experiences and expresses our attitude; it's our mental state as it relates to the world around us. Our mindset provides the basis by which we see life, and how we talk about life and the things we do determine what we accomplish. If we constantly doubt our own thoughts, if we constantly feel we aren't good enough, we will live out those expectations. Therefore, it's incumbent upon leaders to have a positive mindset as we attempt to motivate, influence, and enable others to achieve personal and organizational success.

We "speak" our existence each and every day, and our words shape the world in which we live. It's important we claim, "I am," not "Someday I will be." If we say, "Someday I will be a good leader," our actions will be wrought with hesitation. It leaves people who follow us guessing and wondering if they will be casualties along the journey of our development. But when we have an "I am" mindset—*I am a leader, I am a good leader, I am a great leader*—our actions follow suit. To claim "I am a good leader" doesn't imply the work is done. It's merely a vision of what is and what is to come.

We cannot rely solely on the past. The past is only a foundation. It's a basis from which we can gain *perspective*. We can learn from the past and say, "These are the things that I want to do over again," or "These are the actions I should never take because the result was not positive or effective." Nor can we be so gung-ho for the future that we step over and ignore the present. The only way for the leader's mindset to get to the future is to be in the present. Into this present mindset we incorporate lessons from the past and visions for the future, encompassing all information at our disposal to be effective.

Having a present mindset allows us to claim the "I am." You cannot claim a future for your organization if you are stuck in a mindset that only values past performance. You will never move to that new level of culture called cohesion. When cohesion is present within a team, group, or work environment, performance is present.

## THE FIVE MINDSETS: WHERE DO YOU STAND?

We as leaders prepare our minds through the process of adopting, integrating, and implementing the seven attributes of effective leadership to motivate, influence, and enable others to achieve greatness, first for the one and then the many. With these as a foundation, I offer the following five mindsets. For fun, the mindsets are based on the abilities of superheroes. These are important for leaders of a Cohesion Culture, as mindset influences action.

There's not much point in asking which is more effective; it's sort of like asking someone what his favorite movie is. Be it a hero's journey, some great epic, or a terrific comedy, the answer will vary from person to person, and no answer is the wrong one. Likewise, when it comes to mindset, there's no need to choose only one; each has its time and place. It's often tough to choose just one, and as long as a leader doesn't get stuck in any one mindset, each serves a purpose. When fully engaged, they even work together.

1. **Teleportation.** Of the five mindsets, this is the quickest call to action. It says, "I will," then it stops, assesses, and moves again. Leaders with this mindset focus on growth. They are visionaries who dream big. They put a vision into place and almost instantly create actionable items around that vision. Teleportation types are never lost and rarely, if ever, outsmarted. Ever-hopeful, aggressively far-reaching, even

if what's on their plate seems impossible and elusive, they know with certainty that they will get there. Once they do, it's off to the "next" future. They like to step out on a ledge and lean over the side to see just how far they and their organization can go. Elon Musk, technology entrepreneur, investor, and CEO of SpaceX and Tesla, Inc., tends toward the teleportation mindset. It is as if he's constantly asking, "Are we ready to be bold—to explore strange new lands, new cultures, new ideas, and new ways of being human?"

2.  **Immortality.** This mindset describes leaders who calculate new moves based on what they know today about yesterday. Theirs is a voice of reason based on status quo. Generally speaking, those with an immortality mindset don't seek counsel from others and rely on what they already know. They typically fear that a desired outcome won't be perfect. Leaders with a mindset focused on the past tend to seek perfection rather than a level of performance that's reasonable and acceptable. This mindset says, "I had" but falls short of asking, "Can we think differently? Are we able to work in a space of uncertainty knowing that what we knew then only got us as far as we are now?" Getting to tomorrow requires us to take a leap of faith and become teachable. Make no mistake: it's important to understand the past, as long as we aren't trapped by it. In true immortality fashion, such leaders routinely find themselves doing the same thing over and over again, even when what they're trying to accomplish is a different outcome. To be fair, while it is the most limiting of the mindsets, if you personify immortality as a leader, take heart. When there is turmoil or upheaval or when time is a factor, immortality can lead to sure-fire action, and in these cases, immortality might be just the ticket.

3.  **Empath.** What would it be like to have a totally logical mind
    and be the go-to leader? Leaders with this mindset balance
    what they know with emotional intelligence, saying, "I am,
    I have been, and I will be." The empath mindset embodies
    the ability to assess a present situation and make judgments
    and decisions using both facts and feelings to lead a team.
    It uses intellect to evaluate what's happening and to make
    decisions on multiple levels of thought. Every move these
    leaders make already includes possibilities for the next two
    or three, depending on how a situation plays out. Their
    perspective looks beyond what already exists, and yet they
    are also fully secure in the present moment. Rather than look
    myopically at a situation, they seek a broader vantage point.

    Bill Gates, investor, author, philanthropist, and
    humanitarian, launched Microsoft based on how organizations
    logically interact with programs and processes necessary to
    conduct business. He is quoted as saying, "Success is a lousy
    teacher. It seduces smart people into thinking they can't lose."
    Gates understands the impact of learning and the value of
    bringing fact and feeling together.

4.  **Time Traveler.** The fourth mindset is the bridge that directly
    connects the past with the future. One cannot leap from
    the past to the future without first being in the present.
    Communication mirrors this concept. It connects what
    we already know with what we will learn, say, and do. Our
    communication styles, habits, and preferences open the door
    to what is possible tomorrow, and this inevitably links us to
    what happened before. Leaders with a time traveler mindset
    solve challenges and adapt to opportunities in the here and
    now. They have an open, growth-oriented and teachable
    mind. While acknowledging that a new discovery, innovation
    or piece of knowledge might be valuable in the future, they

maintain a present view and think about how it will help them in the present. Arianna Huffington, Greek-American author, syndicated columnist, and the businesswoman who established Thrive Global in 2007, is a time traveler. She believes communication should go beyond mere awareness and be accessible using today's technology.

5. **Invulnerability.** Who doesn't like the underdog spirit? These tenacious mindset types who keep going for their goal over and over again exhibit an invulnerable "present-simple" mindset. They have perseverance and possess the energy needed to create and sustain a Cohesion Culture. What's happening now, in this moment, matters more than anything else. Leaders with this present-simple mindset dispel naysayers and fight for their employees' hopes, dreams, and aspirations, driving everyone to a future filled with personal and organizational success. Reddit cofounder Alexis Ohanian is of this mindset stock. While Reddit was still in its infancy, his mother was diagnosed with brain cancer. In a 2010 blog post, he summed up this mindset by describing the overall experience thus: "You'd better believe that when you come home to a mother battling cancer and a father spending every waking hour taking care of her and running his own business, you don't complain, you don't cower, and you most certainly don't quit."

Using these leadership mindsets prepares leaders for thinking and creating the ultimate Cohesion Culture. If we are tuned to just one mindset, we will likely restrict which voices we allow and which actions we take. It is unrealistic to believe that a leader will separate how he thinks from how he acts. Within the context of being teachable, the leader will not limit his thinking to just one of the mindsets. Doing so would severely limit his ability to be generative, adaptive and experimental.

In figuring out which mindset is appropriate for either personal or business situations, ask yourself three questions: What are you attempting to accomplish? What do you know about what you want to do? What is possible that you don't already know?

Once a leader evaluates these questions, she is free to choose the mindset that will help produce the best results. When it comes to influencing action, as long as you don't get stuck in one particular mindset, each can benefit the organization.

An example of how a limiting mindset works happened some years ago when my wife drove me to work. We backed out of the driveway and closed the garage door. I noticed my neighbors had their garbage cans sitting out. My wife commented, "It must be garbage day," and suggested that we should put out our garbage can so it would be ready for the trash collectors. I scoffed at this, telling her that garbage day was on Friday, and it was Thursday. I wondered why all of our neighbors had put their garbage out. Because she considered me a trusted voice, I convinced her that I was right and that everyone else on the street had made a mistake.

When I got to my office, I looked at my calendar. To my surprise, it was indeed Friday—garbage day. I had ignored all the evidence of what I saw—all my neighbors' trash cans out on the street—and my wife's trusted, wise counsel for the sake of what I thought I knew. I was convinced I knew more than what others could contribute or teach me.

To identify whether we are limiting our mindset, first we must define the mindset we are working with. We can ask questions like these:

1.  What do I think?
2.  How do I think?
3.  How do I go about the process of thinking?
4.  Am I teachable?
5.  Will I accept other people's viewpoints, especially when they are contrary to my own?

6.  Is there an openness in my mindset to allow for newness and dissension?

It can be hard to answer these questions about yourself, especially if you have never done so before. One of the best ways to challenge the ways in which we limit our mindset is to seek out the voice of others.

## THE VOICE OF OTHERS

*Voice of others = seeking out information that will help you make better and more informed decisions.*

It is paramount leaders understand that in addition to mindset, *outside* factors also sway thinking. I call these factors "the voice of others." But these aren't just anybody's voices. I qualify these as *trusted* voices. These are confidants. These are the people you know will have your back. These are the colleagues and coworkers and individuals who make up your wise council. Your wise council can include business professionals, accountants, lawyers, medical practitioners, social leaders, those who share a similar faith, and family—matriarchs and patriarchs who know you well and who've been on the planet longer.

There is no prerequisite that demands your inner circle have the same perspective as you; theirs may be different than yours, even significantly different than yours. These individuals help you challenge the status quo. They exist to call you out on your sacred cows—any and all ideas, concepts, rituals, traditions, whatever you believe can't be changed.

The voice of others has to do with an individual's consumption of external information. It's important that leaders make conscious decisions as to what they read, see, hear, and say. There are things that cannot be changed, things from which you should never deviate. However, when you find yourself in a position to challenge the status quo, listen to other voices; these trusted voices suggest new concepts and principles. They introduce new ideas and ways of thinking. They help you explore and discuss. They peel back the layers to dig deeper into a subject matter.

Through the process of listening to the voice of these trusted others, we can take a new perspective on our own observations and come up with new possibilities. This can involve visualizing a course of action from something we have seen or experienced in the past. Or we can approach our next action step based on what it could mean for the future. This enables us to, at least in some sense, predict a probable outcome. We can mentally evaluate information for clarity for its application to our final thoughts or ideas that we're looking for, and for logic. This is another opportunity for us to dig deeper, and we should integrate the voice of others into our perspectives to create our final conclusion.

Just remember:

MINDSET (INTERNAL): YOUR OWN VOICE
+ VOICE OF OTHERS (EXTERNAL): YOUR TRUSTED COUNCIL
= ACTIONS: HOW YOU CONDUCT YOURSELF AS A LEADER

## ACTIONS ARE LOUDER THAN WORDS

The final element of influence thinking is concerned with action, specifically the actions of the leader and the group. As I have said before, leadership is the ability of the individual to motivate, influence, and enable others to accomplish something they may not have done on their own. It generates action to accomplish personal and organizational success.

We say actions speak louder than words, but in reality, mindset comes first; what a leader thinks sways her action. The voice of the leader and how she speaks is another form of action. If she has negative thoughts, what comes out likely won't be constructive. If the leader fails to speak words of affirmation and encouragement to others, then the individual may be left feeling that they're not important. Outward recognition, whether it be a friendly greeting, the sound of laughter or a hearty fist bump, are the actions leaders should model to truly create that culture of cohesion. On the other hand, if the leader is fraught with indecision, the result will be indecisive.

## TRANSFORMATIVE PRINCIPLES

This is the final concept the leader must be willing to adopt to bring forth the type of leadership that will be successful in leading a Cohesion Culture. Four specific principles signify the leader's thinking is ready.

Like the seven attributes of effective leaders and the elements of influence thinking, the transformative principles work in tandem. Each of these concepts are independent, yet interdependent upon one another. Let's examine these principles in greater detail:

1.  Aspire to a vision and teach it
2.  Be a good social architect
3.  Create an environment of trust
4.  Practice self-regard

## ASPIRATION VERSUS INSPIRATION

At its core, influence thinking requires a level of trust and collaboration. It circles the bullseye to a sense of belonging to declare: "I am accountable. I instill confidence. I want things to move forward."

The element of action as part of influence thinking includes how we as leaders present and teach vision. When we do not enable employees to gain a sense of belonging and a sense of value so that they feel they can commit to something that is important not only to them but to the organization, they fail. If we expect others to hear our vision once and follow it because we said so, then clearly we do not understand influence thinking. Rather, the vision we communicate must cause those who hear it to *aspire* to greatness, rather than *inspiring* them to greatness. Aspirations are the hopes of achieving something grounded in the reality they can come true, while inspiration is the process of being stimulated to do something.

How do we cause others to aspire to greatness? Primarily by understanding resources and removing barriers that prohibit individuals from achieving their success or the desired outcomes of the organization. Without leaders to guide activity, individuals might not push forward far enough to figure things out. They might not understand that there is more to what they can do. They might not look for any additional information because they aren't aware there is more information to look for. These individuals may need to be challenged to recall observations and things that have been done in the past and project them into the future by asking if they see themselves accomplishing a desired but elusive outcome in another way.

The actions of a leader effectively motivate, influence, and enable others to aspire to greatness far more nobly than what was originally asked for, dreamt, or imagined. Actions that cause others to aspire to greatness do not have to be overly complicated. Outward displays of encouragement assures the team of your confidence in their abilities and promotes a sense of belonging, which is the foundation of a Cohesion Culture.

## BELONGING AND THE IMPORTANCE OF TRUST

Leaders who are smart with people know how to create a trusted environment, which means they have established a safe place for discourse, healthy conflict, and debate. Remember, being a truth seeker is an important leadership attribute. And trust is impossible without a sense of belonging. In the 2019 Edelman Trust Barometer, 77 percent of employees relate how an employer treats them as the highest indicator of trust, and 81 percent of US financial services employees trust their employer to do the right thing.

Leaders of strong trusted environments speak with honesty and candor. Honesty is simply the act of telling the truth, providing all the information—no lies and no omissions. Choosing to leave out critical information is not being honest. Exaggerating information or actions in a way to position people in a better light than they have earned is not being honest.

But leaders must also possess high levels of emotional intelligence. Brutal honesty doesn't create trust either, and it is not the same thing as candor. Trusted leaders take into consideration the way individuals feel and the way they may perceive the information being shared. A major reason people fear change and may hinder cohesion lies within the realm of lack of trust. Sometimes people do not trust change. Distrust creates a disconnect between conflict, communication, accountability, and results that stalls growth. Distrust inhibits the future, as it keeps people trapped in the past, hampering our ability to learn and grow. This lack of trust leads to dysfunction and contributes to an inability to feel a sense of belonging, to see value, and ultimately to make commitments.

So, to create a trusted environment in which all members feel they belong, the transformative leader must possess high levels of emotional intelligence. The social skills that enable leaders to interact with others in a way that creates this sense of belonging easily translate to trust. In that trusted environment, leaders establish a value system of truthfulness among individuals.

## PRACTICE SELF-REGARD

Leaders committed to transformation will inevitably look inward for signs of strengths and weaknesses. It is important for the leader to understand emotional intelligence and to apply it through four common thought processes that denote a specific action: perceive, understand, manage and use emotions to bring about success. Through the art of self-regard, the leader has the capacity and wherewithal to control and express his behavior in meaningful ways.


## LESSONS LEARNED

- Emotional intelligence hinges on self-awareness, maturity, and building rapport with others. It means being motivated by something beyond one's corporate title and, above all else, showing empathy, modeling that it is better to be kind than right.
- Seven attributes encourage cohesion: being teachable, compassionate, grateful, and truth-seeking, and having humility, a pure heart, and the ability to be a peacemaker.
- Leadership is intentional, and what a leader's mind consumes influences how the leader behaves.
- Seeking counsel from wise, trusted voices and being choosy in what voices we listen to are essential in successful leadership.

# CHAPTER 2

# Dance Like Everyone Is Watching

"Leaders must encourage their organizations to dance to forms of music yet to be heard."

**—Warren Bennis, *NY Times* Best-selling Author and Pioneer in Leadership Studies**

**KEY CONCEPTS:**

*1.6* *Belonging:* The sense of fitting in; to have an affinity for a place and a situation.

*1.7* *Transactional leadership:* A leadership style that promotes compliance through rewards and punishments.

*1.8* *Transformative leadership:* A leadership style wherein employees are inspired to succeed out of a sense of collective identity.

I like to think I'm a pretty good dancer, even though I'm not. Regardless, I love to dance. It doesn't matter if I'm familiar with the music, nor does it matter who's watching: if there's a beat and a dance floor, I'm on it. What I lack in rhythm, I make up for in confidence, and I always dance like everyone is watching. My dance skills may need help, but that doesn't stop me.

Even if you've never been that person, you've certainly seen him! The one who is completely in the groove and doesn't care how it looks as long as he's having fun. And somehow he makes other people have fun, too, by instilling some of his confidence in them. They tap into it just watching him show them how it's done.

This is the spirit of the leadership I'm talking about in this book. Leadership is not about being 100 percent right or perfect. Sometimes it means getting people on the dance floor and giving them just the right amount of encouragement to see their passion flow. In fact, anyone who can get someone to the dance floor has just proved he is a leader.

The primary reason I like the dancing analogy for leadership is that as you begin to implement a culture of cohesion, things won't always feel smooth or look good. There will be times when the ensemble is not together and you wonder why in the world you are doing this, and if you'll ever get it right. This is where influence thinking comes into play again: you examine your mindset and adjust it if necessary, you seek out your trusted voice of others, and then you move forward with new action. This is why it takes a leader to implement a Cohesion Culture of belonging, value, and commitment—the culture does not just happen! You don't stop. You keep focusing on the seven leadership attributes that encourage cohesion. You keep creating a culture of trust where people can be themselves and be honest. You use your influence by focusing on the one—getting one person at a time up on the dance floor. And then you get them to dance.

## EVERYONE CAN BE A LEADER

Sometimes people think leaders are only those who have defined followers. People reporting to people is called *explicit leadership*— when an organizational chart puts a formal list of people on it with a defined reporting structure. However, I work from sheet music that says everyone leads regardless of where they are on the charts. It doesn't matter what your role, where you work, or which industry you're in. If someone asks you for advice, direction, or to help, you are performing as a leader. These are *implicit leaders.*

If you think about the values and skills we discussed in the first chapter, you can easily see how it would benefit everyone to personally develop them. We need trusted, wise counsel in our personal lives as well as in business. We could all grow from expanding our mindset; what you put in influences what you put out, positively or negatively, whether in your leadership of a corporation or simply the interactions you have daily with other people. And the ability to influence others positively, toward a greater purpose in their own lives or as part of a collaborative effort, is a great gift in any area of life, both for the influencer and the influenced.

Let's go back to the dance metaphor, but this time in a situation where no one at all is dancing. Maybe the audience is stuffy, or the DJ isn't playing good songs. Maybe no one wants to be the first to take a risk. There's potential for a great time, but the other side of that coin is that you could fail to engage others and just make a fool of yourself. And then it happens. One person decides to take to the floor, then another and another. It's never easy to be the first one dancing, but I'm going to let you in on a little secret: no one really cares how well you dance if you just make the attempt and are willing to learn.

I especially love to see the coaxing that goes into getting folks to the dance floor when it's someone who doesn't like to dance. That can be a real challenge—kind of like helping a person find their purpose when they don't know what to look for. When tempos change, a leader might skip a beat to watch other peoples' moves, but she never interrupts a good groove, and when the music is pumping, she keeps pace. Another challenge is to get the entire crowd moving; to lead a conga line takes a certain skillset. What takes even more skill is choreographing an actual recital. Can you imagine what it takes to execute an entire ballet? To dole out discipline and creativity in equal measure takes a terrific amount of leadership prowess.

Empty dance floors are a great lesson to leaders. Learning new dances is, too. Throughout the history of dance world, there are countless examples relevant to leadership. New dances have been created, like disco, the electric slide, and moonwalking, whose novelty has stood the test of time—for a few generations, anyway. In terms of becoming a good social architect, think of the hokey pokey and how it's inclusive and most anyone can take part. As for creating a trusted environment, one that has potential to lead to organizational transformation, remember the iconic lift in *Dirty Dancing's* climactic scene. That's trust.

Leadership, at its core, is the ability to motivate and influence others to achieve organizational success by doing something they otherwise couldn't do on their own. Remember, as part of implementing a successful Cohesion Culture, leaders must be willing and able to put others ahead of themselves. Consider the leader and his way of thinking and doing for others as a large disco ball glittering in a club. The ball covers the entire floor without being on the floor and lights up the dancers, showing off their moves.

It's important for leaders to understand that their role means asserting a level of personal power that helps talent do what is right because it is right, not because of threats or coercion. In business, this is the only way to ensure a measure will be sustainable. Some people stop short of what they believe their own abilities are; an effective leader helps them carry on. When talent stops looking and acting in a way that achieves greatness, it is usually because they have not looked for additional information or help. The talent may need to be challenged to stop thinking about today and begin acting for tomorrow.

Perspective is important. You might be too wrapped up in the pressure of accomplishing a goal or outcome to see how to tweak your process for success. Take a step back. Listen to the music. Find the rhythm, and with this clarity, get up and dance. We've all heard the expression "The answer is always no if you don't ask." Thankfully, I heeded that advice and found the courage to ask my high school sweetheart to the prom. Because my mind was not trapped in the mindsets of "I am not good enough" or "Someday I will be the perfect date," I have had the privilege to be married to this sweet gal for more than forty years. And just for the record our song was Maxine Nightingale's 1975 international hit "Right Back Where We Started From." This poetic ballad has always been a reminder that no matter what happens, if we stick it out, we'll always return to this wonderful place where it all started. Relating this metaphor to the business world, perspective is how employees are able to access the reasons they first fell in love with the organization.

## LEADERSHIP STYLES

Leadership styles describe mannerisms and the approach the leader takes when motivating, influencing, or enabling others. Leadership styles primarily fall into one of three categories: directive, cooperative, or collaborative.

*Directive*: A directive style informs or tells people what to do. This style is effective when the followers need finite instruction to accomplish a task, like when the dance teacher choreographs the exact steps the dancers will perform to a song she has chosen. Consider also an assembly line wherein workers are required to adhere to a successive order.

*Cooperative*: A cooperative style of leader asks for the input of others yet makes the final decision all on his own. Suppose the dance instructor is open to suggestions from the students as to the type of dance they would like to do next, and to modifications to the choreography. He will listen to the requests and then make the decision alone. A clear illustration of this can be found at a nonprofit where, for example, the organization is looking for advice on how they can impact a community. They'll seek cooperation and have other stakeholders weigh in.

*Collaborative*: When leaders adopt a collaborative style, they tend to lean on an individual or group to make the decision. Under this style, the group chooses the song and makes up the choreography given the established parameters for the desired outcome. A case in point is a typical sales environment. Leaders will incorporate how the team feels they should treat their consumers.

All three leadership styles can be effective depending upon what the goal is. With new or inexperienced dancers, for instance, a directive leadership style will help them become familiar with the basic steps and build confidence as they practice to become better. This is an effective style if you are just beginning the transition to a Cohesion Culture and your employees don't have their footing yet. As their trust builds, both in their ability to know and perform the steps and in you as the dance instructor, cooperative and collaborative leadership styles come into play, enabling dancers to bring their own creativity to the choreography and maybe even make up a new dance.

## TWO THEORIES OF LEADERSHIP

To be clear, leadership theory doesn't necessarily relate to the leadership styles outlined in the previous section. Style is how an individual communicates and commits; theory describes the behavior and how it's communicated to others. You can be transformative and still be directive. Anytime one can put structure to behaviors, it doesn't become accidental; it's purposeful.

Simplified, the transactional theory of leadership is a concept everyone who has ever had a job is familiar with: we go to work and give our time and effort in exchange for a paycheck and possibly other benefits. The employer–employee relationship is based on a transaction in which both participants get something they want.

As familiar as it may sound, however, this is not the only approach to leadership. A newer theory has come into play based on James MacGregor Burns's research comparing transactional leadership with what he called *transformational leadership*. The focus of transformational leadership is change. You may not have heard of transformational leadership before, but you have already become familiar with four transformative principles discussed in Chapter 1.

For further clarity, theories have value and can serve leaders well. Yet many leaders are not only unconscious of which theory they subscribe to, they haven't even heard of them! So, we are going to take a few moments to explore these two theories and their implications.


## TRANSACTIONAL LEADERSHIP

The transactional leader focuses time and attention on the task. Accomplishing a goal is the focus. When leaders are transactional, they initiate solutions that may solve an immediate problem, but the solution is not directed at tomorrow, only today. The transactional leader relates to others based on how well she feels they will be able to complete the task. It is truly a "check box" way to lead. And before you get too cynical about transactional leadership, keep in mind that there are times when being a transactional leader is necessary. For example, in an accounting department, the team is generally focused on specific details—transactions that will result in a balance or final number.

Consider it like a chorus line. The choreographer will insist the moves be perfected by the group and minimize any opportunity for self-expression so as not to distract from the star, who should be the focus of a particular dance. If the audience gets distracted, the entire production could be jeopardized.

But there are plenty of cautions when it comes to transactional leadership. These qualities can be appropriate in specific situations, such as working with employees with whom a strong sense of cohesion already exists to meet a tight deadline or to correct a mistake for a client. But this theory of leadership is not always effective, and rarely so in the long term. So let's consider some characteristics of transactional leadership that can be very effective if used wisely but should be implemented in specific, appropriate situations, and with careful consideration.

A transactional leader often operates from a "silo" mentality, meaning they only think of their own priorities and success and the methods for best accomplishing the goal without considering how those methods might impact employees, positively or negatively.

Also in transactional leadership is the tendency to apply institutional power, which comes from the structure or the hierarchy that a leader is in charge and must be obeyed. This theory of leadership states that individuals will accomplish what needs to be done because the leader has said so and not because they are fully invested and engaged. When it comes to applying institutional powers, one has to keep applying it. The natural tendency when individuals have been forced to do something is to find a way to not do it. However, when the leader applies personal power of influence and helps the employee see the action is the correct course of behavior, then the employee complies and is more likely to repeat the behavior without prompting.

Transactional leadership also expects that those completing a task will bring a certain level of skill they have already developed. In this scenario, the transactional leader is not prepared to spend time adding to employees' skillsets. Teaching, growth, and personal development are not the focus here; results are.

There is also no time for the transactional leader to build relationships. The focus is not on social architecture activities like determining how individuals feel or if they are connecting to the work or whether they understand they are valued. Value lies in completing the task rather than building the employer–talent relationship beyond the extent of offering accolades when the task has been completed to satisfaction. There is a transactional agreement: employees provide their skillset, their time, and their effort, and they receive affirmation for performing a task or completing a goal successfully.

## TRANSFORMATIVE LEADERSHIP

While transactional leadership is needed in specific situations, transformative leadership is essential to a solid Cohesion Culture. A culture of cohesion exists when people say, "I love where I work, I feel the company wants and needs me, and I am willing to do what's needed to get the job done because it is best for me and the company." When this happens, the leader has exerted transformative action supported by influence thinking.

Transformative leaders focus on the needs of others and build goal achievement first through relationships and *then* through tasks. Ensuring that individuals work together in the same organization— whether individually in charge of specific aspects that contribute to a whole or as a group effort—is about teaching vision in a way that causes others to aspire to greatness and fosters a sense of belonging within a trusted environment. The focus is on helping others commit to success; it is off the leader.

When you think of others first, you are working within a collective perspective that utilizes several of the mindsets explained in Chapter 1. The reality is that leaders can motivate others regardless of the intention of their mindset, perspective, or actions. But not all motivation is sourced from a good place. There are leaders who want people to perform because they say so, or in order to get a big raise, or so others will like them. Understandable reasons, certainly, but it begs the question "What are you trying to achieve?" To be the type of leader that champions a Cohesion Culture, we must embody the seven attributes of an effective leader and operate with honesty, compassion, grace, truth, humility, purity of heart, and peace. Then and only then can we understand the transformative power to care about how someone feels and how they are treated.

The opportunity is to think the needs of others outweigh the needs of the individual. There is a dichotomy to it. While a leader must focus on the one, she also ensures there is a collective benefit. Look at it this way: you may individually work with Gretchen, Melinda, Jeff, and Chad, but as a group, they will create a distinct identity; if something isn't working for a single one of them, ultimately you'll need to rethink things. The transformative leader focuses on others by aligning their personal goals with desired organizational outcomes. It's about finding the sweet spot that allows for optimal success because when individuals succeed in what they want to do, the organization will succeed as well. The needs of the individual are meant to be integrated with the needs of the company to access the maximum benefit to both.

To give you an example of this, during an early time in my career I was leading a group of service individuals who handled monetary transactions for a financial institution. One day I noticed one particular rep during an interaction with a customer. I'll call her Charlotte. After cashing a check, Charlotte pulled the money from her drawer and, as was customary, counted the varying denominations to herself first, and then to the consumer. Normally there was nothing out of the ordinary to note about this process, but this time, she brought her leg to the top of her stool and counted the money as she slowly bent the other leg and came back up. She continued this activity, much to the customer's dismay, until the money was given out. This service representative was as nice as could be and always very helpful. The way she counted the money had nothing to do with being considerate or friendly.

After the customer left, I asked Charlotte what she had been doing. Without hesitation or apology, she proudly informed me that one day she was going to be a ballerina. To help her get into shape, she had decided to exercise at various times during the day to strengthen her legs for the rigor needed to perform multiple pirouettes in a row.

This was one of those moments when a leader has to think on his feet. I knew Charlotte had a passion for dancing deep down inside, which I could relate to—although she was obviously much better at it than I was!

It would have been a wonderful ending to this story if I had encouraged her or helped her aspire to be the best ballerina ever. Instead, to my chagrin, I was the transactional leader who told Charlotte that being a ballerina had nothing to do with counting cash and she should stick to what she was being paid to do. My lack of concern for her and her dreams did not lift her up. I became sidetracked in my focus on the transaction rather than on the person. I look back on myself in that moment as a dream stealer, and the saddest thing was, I didn't even know it at the time.

But what would the transformative leader have said in this situation? What I have learned is that I could have acknowledged Charlotte's desire to be a ballerina, to be able to perform perfect lifts and pirouettes and to move flawlessly along the floor on the tips of her toes. Instead of a leader who diminished her dream, she deserved a leader who could first try to see whether that dream could align with the desired corporate outcome of an environment in which customers were comfortable.

Even so, finding such an alignment isn't always possible. In fact, in looking back, I can't see a way for these two desires to align— for Charlotte to perform her strengthening exercises in front of customers while counting money. And yet I still have regrets about how I handled the situation. All would not have been lost if I had looked for a way to motivate, influence, and enable Charlotte to apply the same passion for dancing to being the best serviceperson at our financial institution. I could have acknowledged her dream as important and still helped her to see why her desire to exercise at work was not appropriate. At least she would have had a supervisor who understood how to think of others first.

Even in this case, it's likely I would not have retained Charlotte as an employee. Her personal desire to be the best dancer ever would have aligned perfectly with a dance company that wanted their dancers to perform amazing routines.

In this case, Charlotte leaving her job may sound like an outcome that isn't ideal for my financial institution. And on the surface, it isn't. After all, we spent the money and time to interview, hire, and train Charlotte. But consider this. Where was Charlotte's motivation to put her best into her job going to come from? If she was determined to be a ballerina at all costs, her best efforts would continue to be put toward that goal and not toward improving customer service at work. She might have continued to work for me, and to count money without doing leg exercises, but she would have no incentive to improve, to give above and beyond the minimum of what was asked. At best she would be faking her behavior with customers so as not to get reprimanded by me again.

But if I had been able to address her passion for dancing and communicate that I cared about what was important to her, even if I couldn't accommodate her exercising during customer transactions, I would have invested in an employer–employee relationship that went beyond the transactional. I would have shown Charlotte that I could be trusted to hear her talk about the things that mattered most to her. That I was interested in her whole life, beyond what she could provide my company. That there was room for her to be her true self at work, albeit in an appropriate way. And out of this would likely have come her desire to be the best customer service rep ever. The benefit to a company full of employees like that is self-evident. And *that* is the power of transformational leadership.

In focusing on others, a transformative leader aligns personal goals with desired organizational outcomes; finding that sweet spot allows for optimal success.

## ASPIRING VISION

The word "aspire" means to direct one's hopes or ambitions towards achieving something. Transformative leaders aspire toward a vision that is greater than themselves, and then teach it. The act of teaching the vision is yet another way leaders focus on the needs of others. Teaching allows the vision to be absorbed into the minds and actions of others, and it encourages them to be adaptable and to sustain the vision long after the leader is absent from the group.

Transactional leaders may *inspire* others by filling them with the urge to do something, but simply giving someone motivating reasons to perform or accomplish falls short of transforming them. They have no greater understanding of the vision, which is the true underlying reason to take action. They have no ownership of the vision, because only the leader is in control. This may seem sufficient to achieve an organization's desired outcome, but long-term it limits employee output to the bare minimum—only what is asked of them, only what the leader can imagine to ask.

Leaders who are transformational understand that allowing followers to learn freely and gain insight from self-discovery is more powerful than just telling them what to do. It means they have access to the insight and creativity of their entire team of talent, far beyond what they can come up themselves. Transformational leadership orients toward the future by helping others be their best self in the present.

Another way transformative leaders help others to aspire to their vision is by self-examination and self-correction. These leaders practice self-regard—I like to call it "having that out-of-body experience"—to understand why they did something well so they can model, imitate, and implement the successful behavior again as needed. They also do this to understand what behaviors don't work and why so they can make corrections that ultimately produce a great result from themselves and the individuals they're interacting with.

Part of self-correction is admitting you are wrong. In certain situations, when we realize our actions were not the best, offering an apology can be a powerful example. It is always best to correct yourself before others bring the need to do so to your attention. After asking for forgiveness, move on; there's no need to dwell on your mistakes.

Do understand, though, that when a leader must apologize for his behavior on a regular basis, that leader is not practicing great emotional intelligence. Having emotional intelligence means we know how to work through conflicts, trust others, and keep our own emotions in check without drawing unwanted attention to ourselves. A leader without these traits fails to empathize with others and thinks of himself as more important than others. Ultimately this hurts both the leader and his team, just as if one member of a dancing couple only cares about his moves and does not support his partner unless doing so makes himself look better. Even if he can perform his steps flawlessly alone, if his partner falls out of step and loses the rhythm, the entire dance is interrupted.

## AS ASPIRATION LEADS TO VISION, MOTIVATION LEADS TO PERFORMANCE

Writing for the *Harvard Business Review* in a May 2011 article, "The Power of Small Wins," American academics Teresa Amabile and Steven J. Kramer, who for over two decades have studied psychological experiences and the performance of people doing complex work inside organizations, offered, "The power of progress is fundamental to human nature, but few managers understand it or know how to leverage progress to boost motivation." How can something that's central to what it means to be human be so elusive at the same time?

Early in Amabile and Kramer's work, they realized that "a central driver of creative, productive performance was the quality of a person's inner work life—the mix of emotions, motivations, and perceptions over the course of a workday." How happy workers feel; how motivated they are by an intrinsic interest in the work; how positively they view their organization, their management, their team, their work, and themselves—all of these combine either to push them to higher levels of achievement or drag them down. An important aspect of building cohesion is helping the employee feel valued. Leaders instill confidence in their team when they help employees connect the dots. In other words, employees' inner selves are fueled with the knowledge that what they do matters. Amabile and Kramer's work supports the assertion that "buying" engagement does not last. It is superfluous and at best only produces a temporary form of employee commitment.

Amabile and Kramer studied twenty-six project teams from seven companies and 12,000 diary entries from 238 individuals. Their goal was to discover the states of inner work life and workday events that correlated with the highest level of creative output. They propound,

> In a dramatic rebuttal to the commonplace claim that high pressure and fear spur achievement, we found that, at least in the realm of knowledge work, people are more creative and productive when their inner work lives are positive—when they feel happy, are intrinsically motivated by the work itself, and have positive perceptions of their colleagues and organization. Moreover, in those positive states, people are more committed to the work and more collegial toward those around them. Inner work life, we saw, can fluctuate from one day to the next— sometimes wildly—and performance along with it. A person's inner work life on a given day fuels his or her performance for the day and can even affect performance the *next* day.

Once they figured out this "inner work life effect," they turned to whether and how a leader could set it in motion. If inner work life drives performance with consistent headway, something happens. Amabile and Kramer called this something a "progress loop"; rather than managing people, organizations were better served when leaders managed progress.

Based on these findings, it's clear that leaders should be invested in creating an environment in which employees' inner work life can thrive. Having a positive inner work life involves exactly the elements of belonging, value, and commitment central to Cohesion Culture. In the next section we'll investigate *why* this inner work life provides so much motivation, and how leaders can be effective in motivating others.

## THE THREE ELEMENTS OF MOTIVATION

Why do we do what we do? How do we motivate others to do what we want them to or what we see as the best course of action? What are the needs, desires, wants, or driving forces behind the actions of others? All of these elements can be summed up in the term *motivation*. Through motivation, people encourage others and themselves to accomplish goals, objectives, or to simply perform a task. But do we really understand what motivates us? And if so, do we understand what motivates other people?

According to David McClelland, author of the 1961 book *The Achieving Society*, there are three elements of motivation:

1. Affiliation
2. Achievement
3. Power

Individuals are highly motivated when they affiliate, a form of attachment in which people are inclined to connect or be in association with others or with an entity. Affiliation is the act of joining forces, aligning, or in some instances combining. It's *belonging*, in cohesion terms. When individuals form a group, they invest a portion of their identity into what is called the *group mentality*—just a fancy term for describing how a group thinks and acts to handle typical, day-to-day activities. People have a need to be part of something. Belonging offers value because it gives people purpose, and passion is the emotional joy from exercising one's purpose.

Second, McClelland discusses motivation from the perspective of achievement. This parallels the two other components of the cohesion construct: value and commitment. Achievement connects how someone accepts or expresses value and the level of commitment they are willing and able to make. Individuals derive value when they feel accomplished. Goal. Done. Check. There's a feeling of pride.

Now we move on to the third element of motivation, power. McClelland suggests that a leader or higher authority can use either institutional or personal power. Institutional power is the formal authority that comes with a hierarchical regime and is applied as such. Personal power is the ability to persuade or influence people to do something because they feel it is the right thing to do. When leaders have to instruct others to do something with the expectation of performance, the effects are more likely to be short-lived than when the power applied is personal.

McClelland's research on power brings the Cohesion Culture concept full circle. Leaders who focus on doing what is right because it is right create a positive environment that can be sustained for long periods of time.

When considering the aspects of a Cohesion Culture alongside McClelland's theory of motivation, we have a perfect dance couple, sort of like Fred Astaire and Ginger Rogers.

As a leader, what drives me is being able to affect others—to help them find their purpose and sense of belonging. If on a corporate level I am seen as a producer, that's fine, but it's being a director that really gets my fingers snapping. Sure, there's the strategic objectives, financials, the day-to-day operations, the marketing, the whole of what it means to keep a business afloat, but when my vision sparks someone else's excitement, that's when I hear music.

This is why Cohesion Culture is so important to me. It's that toe-tapping, head-bobbing beat where everyone is having a good time, and everyone is glad they made it to the party. Cohesion means helping people with their moves so they can be good and, more importantly, feel good. It's also about coming together to dance, learning the moves and showing what you can do with an air of commitment that says, "I am taking home the trophy."

Alas, I may never be proficient at the waltz, but I do a killer chicken dance. I tried to learn the Charleston once. Took formal dance lessons to try and shake up the old bones. Thought it might be sort of cool to do a dance named after my hometown, the harbor city of Charleston, South Carolina. Back in the 1920s it was a mainstream hit popularized by composer/pianist James P. Johnson. It originated in the Broadway show *Runnin' Wild* and became an overnight hit.

Some sources link the dance back to part of an African-American dance called Juba. This dance seemed perfect for me because the first step is a simple twisting of the feet, something I completely understand. But the dance evolved, and when it got to Harlem, a kicking step both forward and backward were added; then, to add more intrigue, someone decided to include a tap.

What inspires me about this dance is how it started simple and became more complex. It incorporated new moves and sequences with each evolution. That's how leaders create cultures of cohesion. They do it in bite-sized pieces, adding layers upon layers with the intention of helping others to find their purpose and a sense of belonging, and to have value and commit to meaningful work and desired outcomes.

No day passes that, given health and sustenance, we shouldn't celebrate all it means to be alive, vital, and part of something bigger than ourselves. Each day, we should strive to evolve and be an even better version of our self.

When we encourage diversity and invite everyone to the dance floor, the office might be more of a mosh pit than line dance, but in asking everyone to boogie, we ensure a sense of belonging. We make it clear what matters. To solve today's problems, the perfect pirouette must tango with a foxtrot.


## LESSONS LEARNED

- Everyone can be a leader. If someone asks you for advice, direction, or to help, you are performing as a leader.
- There are three leadership styles—directive, cooperative, or collaborative—that can be effectively implemented based on the situation and people involved.
- Transformational leadership is the key to creating a Cohesion Culture.
- People are motivated by forming an attachment with others (belonging), by gaining a sense of accomplishment through achievement (value and commitment), and by the use of personal power (influence thinking).

# Act 2:
# Build the Culture

# CHAPTER 3

# *People Seek to Belong*

"We cannot change what we are not aware of, and once we are aware, we cannot help but change."

—Sheryl Sandberg, author, COO at Facebook and founder of Leanin.org

**KEY CONCEPTS:**

1.9     *Organizational intelligence:* This simple process corresponds to an organization's culture to refer to an organization's ability to mobilize all of its available brainpower.

1.10    *Locus of control:* This concept communicates the extent of power employees feel they have over their workplace experience.

Imagine you're in a foreign country, someplace you've never been. Imagine that everything you're wearing, tasting, hearing, seeing—all of what you're experiencing—is just a little different from what you are accustomed to—maybe even a lot different. The language is unfamiliar. The social norms are confusing. It may take you a while, days, weeks, months, in some cases even years, to get the hang of things.

When what surrounds us is alien, we tend to cling to the familiar. We find ourselves trying to, if not assimilate, at least make an attempt to fit in. This isn't to say we don't enjoy being special and standing out, be it for our keen wit, our winning smile, or the fact that we're willing to be the first one on the dance floor, but it isn't until we have a sense of belonging that any of us perform at our fullest potential.

In order to feel we belong, however, we need something to belong to. This is where culture comes into play in an organizational setting. When organizations value retention, they put effort and energy into their culture. Culture refers to a shared system of thinking. It's the norms, traditions, rituals, customs and symbols that reflect the values, beliefs, attitudes and behaviors of the community that shares the culture. These primary characteristics, when added together, define an organization's culture.

One big indicator of culture is attitude. An organization's attitude come from its core values and the belief system shared by all the people who work there. Fundamentally, the organization must establish a core value system as a basis of operation. Within this, the organization determines the amount of risk it's willing to take and its attention to innovation. This then determines whether its orientation is toward people and people development or toward completing a process or task.

An organization's culture is sometimes called *organizational intelligence*, and just like regular intelligence, it doesn't happen in a vacuum. It's formed in two ways. First, an organization's senior-most members—referred to as the C-suite but also including tenured employees—are responsible for it. Second, individuals within the organization are indoctrinated and socialized in the various ways in which the organization is described; these "definitions" or "norms" include customs, habits, and rituals that are passed along from one employee to another. When norms are established and repeated, we have culture.

A culture's success is determined by how truthfully it's articulated and expressed by its members. Honesty creates a layer of transparency. People see it. They understand it. They know it.

Leaders act on it. When it comes to organizational intelligence and culture, sameness isn't important, or at least it shouldn't be, but in building Cohesion Culture, nothing is more powerful than leaders advocating a sense that every constituent of the culture belongs.

## THE CORE OF COHESION

The core of Cohesion Culture rests on the innate human need to belong. In Maslow's hierarchy of needs, belonging is third only to basic physiological needs, like food and water, and the need for safety. Therefore, it's not surprising that people look to belong in a workplace environment and not just in their personal lives. Social connections are extremely powerful; they have universal appeal and aren't restricted to a single culture or geographical area of the world. This connection influences emotions and the way we think.

Oftentimes, individuals express self-esteem through the actions and words they extend to other team members. These social behaviors offer insight into an employee's sense of belonging, value, and commitment. When individuals exchange information with each other, through greetings and niceties, social exchange is happening. Organically, they create a value system that exchanges information or exchanges action for action. With laughter and the freedom to enjoy informal interaction, they demonstrate their sense of belonging. These social behaviors are extremely important in creating cohesion.

Organizations wanting to create a sense of belonging within different groups must find ways to validate the group as an important part of the organization. Validation strengthens relationships among individuals. Validation, recognition, and acceptance of the individual can signify not only that the individual belongs to the organization but also that they are contributing value. Individuals see this validation of the value they bring as an essential part of their acceptance into a group. This is why it's so important for leaders to help followers to see value in what they do. This is where the whole becomes more than just the sum of its parts.

So culture depends, first and foremost, on an employee's sense of belonging. Culture is a combination of how individuals react socially and whether or not they achieve a sense of unity through social behaviors. Leaders can look toward the organization's core values to establish a basic framework from which the organization will operate when all of the individuals within the organization align themselves to belong.

## DEFINING CORE VALUES

A high-performing Cohesion Culture has defined values that are easily understood and replicated. The organization operates within a realm that's morally, ethically, and legally acceptable to the group. We know that a Cohesion Culture can make that happen because in that near-perfect environment, the individuals believe they belong. They are valued and feel that they bring value to the organization. They know that the work they're doing is meaningful. They understand that what they do connects with other pieces of the organization, as well as with other employees and their actions. The cohesive culture provides an opportunity for individual success, in addition to organizational success. When employees make this commitment to themselves and the success of the organization, they operate in a synchronized way that leads to high performance within the culture. The ideal organizational culture works harmoniously with individuals of congruent mindsets. It provides the opportunity for the individual to perform, not for the individual to be perfect.

Because individuals gain a sense of belonging when they can align with others' value systems, it's important for an organization to establish strong values that individuals can then relate to. An individual's belief systems manifest in how they choose to see themselves, the role they play in their service to others, the level of persistence they apply to a particular situation, their level of efficacy, which contributes to whether they can be successful or not, and their belief in making lasting connections and why that is important.

Core values always need to be defined clearly and specifically so that individuals understand what those values mean within the context of the organization. There are three general core values that are helpful in stimulating Cohesion Culture. They are discipline, integrity, and honesty. Below I will give examples of each and how you might define them within an organizational context.

Discipline encompasses so many important traits. Discipline requires that leadership define what the organization's standards are: What are the particular actions individuals need to take? Then we move on to the level of diligence people display: Are they reliable, dependable? Can you count on them? This might lead to accountability as another core value—individuals taking responsibility for their actions.

Integrity is the second core value that distinguishes the way individuals operate in Cohesion Culture. It can be defined in many ways in an organizational setting. For instance, it could refer to always giving your best in any situation. It could mean admitting when you've made a mistake, or being willing to ask for help when you need it.

This is a good example of why it's important to define your core values. If employees know that integrity is one of your company's core values and that it means asking for help when they don't understand something or have taken on too much, then they will know what action to take instead of wondering what to do and feeling insecure.

The third core value is honesty. Honesty at its most basic means being truthful, but the organization should provide specifics so that employees don't assume, for instance, that choosing to leave out critical information is technically being honest because they didn't lie. Honesty in the workplace means there is no omission of fact. One doesn't leave out information to look better. In the same light, exaggeration or misrepresentation falls into the category of dishonesty as well. Also, it might be helpful to address whether it's possible to be *too* honest by offering information that isn't helpful or necessary and that hurts someone else.

## ALIGNING VALUES

Leaders play an influential role in aligning the core values of individuals with those of the organization to ensure there is congruency of words and deeds.

Let's walk through how this alignment occurs. First the leader specifies a value that reflects how individuals within the organization should think and act. For instance, if honesty is the value, we would first need to define what encompasses exhibiting honesty. This might be as simple as clarifying that the people within the organization should tell the truth in all dealings with individuals and other entities.

Next, each individual agrees to abide by this definition and ensure that his or her individual choices relating to truth are aligned with all policies, procedures, communications, and agreements.

With values now aligned, the leader sets expectations for requiring or anticipating projected outcomes. Again, for the individual to commit fully, there must be congruency of expectation and reward so that one doesn't outweigh the other. Then and only then can leader and employee reach a level of consensus that establishes group agreement.

Communicating core values clearly helps employees comprehend expectations for behavior and consequences as a representative of the organization. In aligning core values with these expectations comes the interpretation of value called *locus of control.*

## LOCUS OF CONTROL

Locus of control deals with responsibility. People who blame circumstance for their troubles rather than the personal choices they make are generally weak in character, self-absorbed, and unwilling to be accountable. So, it behooves leaders to foster a workplace environment with a high locus of control.

Leaders have, unsurprisingly, significant influence over whether their employees feel empowered or disempowered in the workplace. Empowerment is more than just a feel-good idea. Employees who feel empowered take responsibility for their work and their mistakes rather than trying to pass the buck. When it comes to how much power employees feel they have over their workplace experience, and where they feel power resides, understanding locus of control can help.

Locus of control is concerned with internal versus external factors and deals with how the individual assigns value to self (high locus) or to circumstance (low locus). High locus of control means that the individual believes the choices one makes in life determine how one is seen and valued. Individuals with low locus of control, then, consider circumstances to provide the stimulus for their individual behavior.

To further illustrate the locus of control concept, let's use the circumstance of a flat tire making you late for work. There are two ways to approach this situation. Sometimes, of course, we blow a tire unexpectedly and can't help but be late. But sometimes we are able to predict and avoid the possibility of a flat tire. A warning light comes on in your car to tell you that the air pressure is low. Or maybe you drove through a construction zone; you would be wise to check for nails in your tire. If your tires are old and the tread has worn down, it's a good idea to regularly inspect your tires for leaks, or to replace them.

If we do not heed these signals and then get a flat tire, producing a consequence like being late for work, the individual with a low locus of control blames the flat tire for this result. But the individual who acknowledges his own choice to ignore the signals demonstrates a high locus of control. He accepts responsibility for being late for work instead of blaming it on the circumstance of getting a flat tire. Likely he will learn from this experience and not make the same mistake twice. In fact, people with a high locus of control are less likely to make mistakes like this because they understand that their actions and choices directly influence outcomes in their life and the lives of those around them. These are the kinds of people you want in your organization. They are trustworthy, they have integrity, and they exhibit discipline—the basic core values that should be part of your organizational culture.

## PEOPLE ARE LIKE TREES

I use a simple analogy that employees are like trees. They start as seedlings, and when nurtured and cared for, they grow to become trees—in some instances, very tall trees. Employees with tenure have a great level of organizational intelligence. They know things about how the organization works, how people interact, and how to get things done that cannot be conveyed in a policy, procedure, or documented desk job aid. We want these trees to stay in the forest.

One way we care for our trees is with human resources strategies and practices. Individuals working in HR are champions of people. They reflect employee voices and help leaders work through myriad red tape and complicated legislation to ensure the work environment is safe and sound for all who enter.

From personal experience, I know South Carolina Federal Credit Union spends a considerable amount of time and money putting initiatives in place that are designed to make employees love where they work. The strategy is to retain employees. Everything hinges on this concept. These HR strategies and practices align, balance, and actively administer employee-related functions, such as talent acquisition;

onboarding; salary administration; benefits; mental, physical, and financial well-being initiatives; relational and social connectivity; performance development; evaluation; and talent retention.

The hope is these programs help make a strong emotional connection between employee and employer—and that it's enough of a connection to keep employees feeling like they belong. When employees no longer feel connected to the organization, they begin to consider an exit strategy.

But even when an organization succeeds in creating a Cohesion Culture, there are any number of life events—from spousal transfers to military assignments to divorce to retirement—that cause our trees to leave. This requires that a replacement be found for the tree, and almost without exception, every hiring manager wants a new *tree*—they don't want a seedling or a sapling to take the place of the full-grown sequoia or the live oak. They want a mammoth, a large-trunked evergreen ready to step into the space once occupied by a root system the size of a car.

Unfortunately, finding that tree is nearly impossible, and so the best option is to replace our tree with a seedling. Now, you may ask, why is this important here? How does having an employee leave impact belonging? Because this organizational event disrupts the timing of belonging. It shifts the dynamics of the work team, the culture, and the potential outcomes already planned for and promised—especially when an organization is trying to build a culture of cohesion.

Therefore, handling new talent correctly is of paramount importance. The following story offers a great illustration of how South Carolina Federal onboards new talent.

On a trip to the Philippines, I learned how cacao (pronounced ka-cow) trees are prepared. Until it is about nine months old and begins to produce the very first part of a tree, a seedling is nurtured. To ensure that it produces rich chocolate, as soon as the lush, green leaves appear, they are snipped. What's left is a stalk. The stalk is then slit, and a piece of mature cacao tree is grafted to it.

I was told that left to its own accord, a cacao tree would take five years to produce fruit, but grafting an older tree to a sapling allows the tree to produce chocolate in two years. Grafting reduces the amount of time and energy a seedling needs to become a fully productive tree by well over 50 percent.

This is how I think of the relationship between a leader and a follower. The notion of belonging can be greatly impacted when a seasoned employee spends time with a new seedling. This process exemplifies how leadership and the champions of people work together to strengthen the culture and create moments of cohesion. Taking the example further, it illustrates the tight-knit relationship between our champions of people in HR and the people themselves.

## CULTURE CHAMPIONS

As you'll discover in Chapter 6, the human resource strategies and practices support the overall cohesion culture and the talent retention model. In the context of belonging, those individuals working in our human resources division are affectionately known to me as "Champions of People."

Human resources works with leadership, and together they are the keepers of the culture. These HR professionals serve as advocates of people and culture both at the boardroom table and in the hallways. With every strategy and tactic, they shout to the employee base, "You matter. You belong. You are valued." People get a sense of being part of the organization when someone takes the time to make it a priority.

But the HR department cannot and for the most part does not want to do it alone. They want leadership to take the new hire, be it seedling, sapling, or tree, and plant it firmly within the organization's framework. Feed it and nurture it. Keep it around for years to come. Make sure the tree knows it has a place where it belongs.

## LESSONS LEARNED

- When an organization values retention, it puts effort and energy into creating a culture or shared system of thinking that contains core values.
- Three essential core values for stimulating Cohesion Culture are discipline, integrity, and honesty.
- People with a high locus of control take responsibility for making choices that increase or decrease the probability of a desirable outcome rather than blaming circumstances.
- Leaders have a responsibility to "graft" their experience onto newer employees by spending time developing them.

# CHAPTER 4

# *The Mary Poppins Effect*

"Today, power is gained by sharing knowledge, not hoarding it."

**—Dharmesh Shah, author, co-founder and CTO of HubSpot**

## KEY CONCEPT:

1.11    *Learning organization:* A business or entity wholly aligned to seeking and using knowledge, adapting to change and allowing employees to make mistakes through controlled experimentation.

My fascination with Mary Poppins began in 1964 at the Robinson Grande Theatre in Clarksburg, West Virginia. It was my first big-screen event, and I would not sit anywhere but the front row. Our next-door neighbor, Susan Cork, took me. It was one of my first times in the big city without Mom or Dad. I was like a kid in a candy store, checking out everything I saw. When the movie appeared on the screen, I could not believe it. Holy cow, Batman; the images were bigger than life! Just Ms. Cork and me, some popcorn, and a drink.

Throughout this narrative, we've talked a good deal about Cohesion Culture's cornerstones: a sense of belonging, values, and commitment. But our work isn't done. Cohesive cultures have other dynamics. These "layered undercurrents" are what allow creativity and promote innovation; they're also where organizational solutions wait. In this chapter, with a little help from Mary, I describe what it means to be a learning organization and offer insights from pioneers in management and systems theory as well as my trusted colleagues at South Carolina Federal.

An organization's capacity to learn commands its future. Knowledge is power. With knowledge, people can make well-informed decisions. Taking time to learn is an important aspect of being teachable. As we learn, we must relax. Take it in. Don't be in a rush. Create a rhythm of absorbing knowledge almost as though you are playing a piano and must keep time with a metronome. You want to use information as if it's what's keeping tempo. In other words, the key is utilizing what's been learned rather than suffering paralysis by analysis. Information doesn't do anyone any good if it isn't used.

Mary Poppins is a teacher at heart, and that's where she and I merge. Pretty much everything any of us need to know about leading a learning organization can be discovered in *Mary Poppins* and *Mary Poppins Returns*. I call the insight she offers to leaders the Mary Poppins effect. She shows us that laughter can cure almost anything, that we should always take time to fly a kite, and above all else that even a world full of responsibilities can be beautiful and fun.

## THE FIVE KEY PRACTICES OF LEARNING ORGANIZATIONS

Learning organizations promise an environment where employees can challenge the status quo. They are safe spaces where the goal is to learn, not just produce results. They are often incubators where creative solutions are encouraged to develop and grow.

American systems scientist Peter Senge, designated as the strategist of the century by the *Journal of Business Strategy*, tells us a learning organization is necessary to initiate change. A former lecturer at the MIT Sloan School of Management and founding chair of the Society for Organizational Learning, Dr. Senge is best known for his book *The Fifth Discipline*, which first introduced the concept of a learning organization.

Peter Senge's five key practices provide leaders a framework. Learning organizations—ones that seek to reshape how they exist in the marketplace—must be generative, adaptive, and willing to experiment. Diversity is another necessity; employees cannot be distracted by external biases that will restrict information. You never want what you see on the outside to distract you from what's on the inside. Lastly, organizations must be good stewards of organizational resources; they must think like a designer and a teacher.

1.  **Generative.** Organizations that are generative have an insatiable appetite to gain knowledge. When Mary Poppins sings to young John, "It's good to know you're bright, for intellect can wash away confusion," ultimately her goal is to get him to use his imagination. But her advice makes it clear that brains are designed to research and investigate. In countless sectors and myriad industries, economists acknowledge "skill" gaps that can be bridged by people working out of generative organizations.

    **Takeaway:** In order to figure things out, solve problems, and stay relevant, we need to learn.

2.  **Adaptive.** Life is full of changes. Being adaptive means the organization has the ability to reshape and then innovate. Rather than resist when the wind changes direction, Mary Poppins unfurls her umbrella and sets a new course. Famously, she "stays until the door opens." Being adaptive

doesn't mean changing simply for the sake of changing; these organizations change for the sake of the future and the potential to be gained. Being adaptive means overcoming our fear of change. Our fears keep us from innovating, which means fear inhibits the future. Fear stops us from adapting to a new way of thinking or creating a new process because we cannot see how the change could be good. Leaders must be willing to step up and make tough decisions.

**Takeaway:** Instead of fighting and fearing change, we need to embrace the change and learn from our fears about it.

3. **Experimental.** One of Mary Poppins' best quotes is "It's fine for life to get a bit messy." And this is how learning organizations approach experimentation. There is nothing that a little twine and tape can't mend. My dad would be proud to know that while I might not have been in the garage for a greasy oil change when I was younger, today I can do some pretty darn good fixing with duct tape.

**Takeaway:** It's impossible to implement effectively without experimentation, and experimentation means making mistakes and messes along the way.

4. **Diversity.** Mary Poppins opens the children's eyes to new experiences. She jumps into chalk drawings, talks to animals, grows and shrinks, and travels around the world in nanoseconds. While Elon Musk might globetrot in the blink of an eye, such experiences are out of reach for most leaders. But diversity isn't. Introducing followers to unique experiences and opening their eyes to new concepts and ideas has a huge positive impact on an organization. Challenging followers to think outside of the box and to recognize as well as accept innovative solutions helps a company to stay on the cutting

edge. What I find especially interesting about this element is that Senge did not refer to diversity as many of us traditionally think of it—based on an individual's race or nationality, gender preference, or sexual orientation. Diversity is about including diversity of thought, without those extrinsic biases that affect what we hear, what we interpret, and what we learn.

**Takeaway:** When we accept the views of others, we build a level of influence thinking that says, "I will listen for what I do not know."

5.  **Stewardship.** Mary Poppins doesn't just tell the children what to do. She invests in teaching them values as simple as cleaning up after themselves and apologizing. As a result, not only does their love and respect for her build, but they are also able to repair and rebuild their relationship with their parents. Leaders have an opportunity to be good stewards. Individuals are our most important resources—that's why it's called "talent" acquisition and retention. When we enable individuals, we are being good stewards of our resources. Remember, leadership is about inspiring a vision larger than the leader and then teaching it to others. As teachers, leaders provide the opportunity for a little old something I like to call *self-discovery*.

    **Takeaway:** People are our most valuable resources, and we must take the time to build relationships, create an environment of trust, and align others' needs with organizational outcomes.

Is it possible for us to turn back time to when we were young? Can we retreat to that child-like openness and freedom to take on new information? We were adaptable as children. Never met a person we didn't like, never walked away from a challenge, at least the first time.

Our ability to grow and adapt is part of our survival. We gain confidence when we learn. Information improves our chances of getting it right the first time. Mary Poppins was a wonderful designer, teacher, and good steward of resources. She had a unique, funny way of helping the children adapt to change through experiences. Life is a great teacher when we open our minds and get out of the way.

## SYSTEMS AND CHANGE

Peter Senge indicates that organizations face four challenges in initiating change.

1.  There must be a compelling reason for change.
2.  There needs to be appropriate time to make the change.
3.  There must be help during the change process.
4.  Do not let a new problem not before considered important or perhaps not previously recognized become a critical barrier to the process of change.

John Kotter, the Konosuke Matsushita Professor of Leadership, Emeritus, at the Harvard Business School and a well-known thought leader, has an interesting connection with Senge's four challenges of change. In Kotter's eight-step change model, he too begins with creating a sense of urgency; he includes the importance of developing a vision and timeline, creating a coalition of support, and removing obstacles that impede change. Kotter further advises celebrating the small wins, building on the change, and staying the course. We can learn a great deal from these two leaders.

People resist change for a variety of reasons. One is a lack of belief. They don't believe that the change is necessary, so they do not believe that the change will make any difference in what they're doing. In mitigating these challenges of change, Dr. Senge offers systems thinking. His five disciplines include shared vision, systems thinking, mental models, team learning, and personal mastery.

This is why putting the practices of a learning organization in place is necessary to create a Cohesion Culture. Many organizations that I have spoken with around the globe do not even know if they truly have cohesion. A Top-500 executive admitted, "The strategies and practices we put in place are lame or at best non-existent."

Unfortunately, we want employees to get along and commit to doing a good job with little or no effort on our part. We have been lulled into believing that because people have a need to belong, it just magically happens. Based on my experience and the tales of woe from those I consult with, it takes more than just a visit from a nanny blown in from the east with a neatly pinned hat, properly tailored overcoat, fanciful umbrella, and never-ending carpet bag of goodies.

**Shared vision.** The bridge to creating value is a shared vision. A shared vision is one in which every employee within an organization takes part. This helps to alleviate anxieties and uncertainty about change and gives individuals an opportunity to live it, breathe it, and own it. When individuals know what the big picture is, they have an opportunity to self-correct if things get off track or to make necessary changes so their tasks are integrated for the benefit of a shared outcome.

**Systems thinking.** From a holistic viewpoint, systems thinking allows organizations to look for patterns that can help change, help growth, remove obstacles, and move individuals and the organization toward better development. Such thinking not only focuses on individual concerns but also reflects the view of the organization as a whole. You might say that the needs of the many outweigh the needs of the one. (Yes, I just quoted *Star Trek*.) With influence thinking, we look at people individually, but we must focus on them as a part of the whole. This also correlates nicely to the quote I often repeat, "You cannot serve the many until you serve the one." Applying systems thinking and influence thinking simultaneously allows us to focus on the individual, and then the "many"—the systems and processes that surround what those individuals are doing.

**Mental models.** Mental models deal with individual mindsets and enable individuals to visualize what the company is about and where it's going. A mental model of adaptability allows the organization and its employees to be flexible in the solutions and the innovation they bring forward. These mental models provide a potential image of the company in the future, and according to Dr. Senge, the most successful companies are those that can learn and adapt to new models in order to become faster than the competition.

**Team learning.** It is important for the workforce to consider all of their colleagues as contributors, not as competition. In team learning, the collaborative mindset sets the tone for individuals to be vulnerable and transparent as they operate within their task, within their responsibility, to achieve the outcome delineated by the organization. Transformative leadership behavior focuses on aligning optimal outcomes for the individual with the organization's goals. This type of team dynamic requires the sense of belonging, the opportunity for the team to establish a mental identity, and, more specifically, for individuals to understand what the dynamics of the group will look like when everyone functions together.

**Personal mastery.** Personal mastery deals with how individual employees prepare for goals, objectives, and activities, as well as their perception of reality, of the organization's vision, and of others within the organization. Within the realm of personal mastery, individuals adopt a shared vision of the organization, look at the big picture from a systems perspective, and create mental models that allow for increasingly robust, critical, and integrative thinking even when they hold opposing ideas in their mind at the same time.

## HOW LEARNING DIRECTS FUTURE SUCCESS

Our girl Poppins quips, "Everything is possible, even the impossible." Mary looks at goals and objectives from the vantage point that anything goes. Her eclectic view on life asserts that when the world turns upside down, the best thing to do is turn right along with it. My all-time favorite line of hers is "When you change the view from where you stood, the things you view will change for good."

Organizations that fail to employ a learning mindset might take care of the task at hand, but they won't have the staying power for long-haul, far-reaching success. An organization that survives the day-to-day grind by being reactionary in its response to change or turmoil works from what is called a *single-loop mindset*. This organization corrects the information to reflect only the change needed for the moment. *Double-loop learning* takes things a step further by asking, "How will this change impact me in the future? What are future policies, procedures, training? What are the other elements that the organization needs to think of from a strategic standpoint?"

For instance, if an employee omits a crucial step in a production process, such as a quality control review, the single-loop mindset will perhaps require that a manager check every time to make sure the QC review has occurred. This certainly is one way to address the problem, and it may reduce the likelihood of the quality control review being forgotten, but it has several negatives: it adds busywork for the manager, and it disempowers employees, taking the responsibility for the production processes away from them. In addition, it doesn't get to the reason *why* this step was forgotten.

The double-loop mindset will investigate this. It asks, "Is this a one-time error, or does it reflect a lack of familiarity with the production processes that reveals a problem with our training program? What will the impact be of having a manager check up on employees in charge of QC? Will this begin to shift too much responsibility and too much power to the manager, ultimately causing her other responsibilities to suffer? Will it create a mindset that employees don't really have to be responsible for their own work because their manager will come along behind them to make sure they haven't forgotten anything?" The double-loop mindset looks at the problem holistically, ultimately discovering in this case that a weak spot in the training program is impacting quality control.

A double-loop mindset combines structure and strategy for optimal outcomes. An organization's culture is its structure, the conceptual ideal that forms the framework for how people interact in the environment. The strategy is the overarching vision for the future of the organization. In this book, I present Cohesion Culture as the structure and talent retention as the strategy.

## STRUCTURE AND STRATEGY

Combining structure and strategy is viewed by 72 percent of surveyed organizations as having increased success and profitability. Leaders within these organizations claim they will be able to reduce operational cost as a result.

One way to align structure and empower a strategic mindset is to flatten the hierarchy of the organization. This "flattening" reduces barriers that might otherwise restrict communication among team members, increases the benefits of "cross-functional" teams and aids them in finding resolutions. With the creation of cross-functional teams, organizations garner collaborative viewpoints from individuals who have different levels of experience and specialized knowledge, as well as organizational intelligence.

*Cross-functional* means that team members can move from one team, department, or assignment to another. This kind of fluidity and flattening of hierarchy has a direct positive impact on performance; individual teams within an organization might compare themselves to each other, but they do not consider other teams as competitors keeping them from achieving the ultimate goal of personal and organizational success. They understand that all individuals are working toward a common goal, although they may go about it differently—expressing different feelings or adopting different behaviors.

In addition, this cross-functionality creates great adaptability within an organization, as team members are intimately familiar with multiple aspects of a process or assignment. Everyone is essential, but the absence of one person doesn't throw a wrench into the gears. Someone else can easily fill in for them. This levels the playing field and ensures that everyone on the project is an MVP.

In this way, the learning organization allows for the individuals within that company to work toward growth and development. If the organization wants to employ a strategy of learning, then the culture must be aligned in a way to make that happen. Culture is the foundation, the building blocks from which strategy moves forward.

## THREE EFFECTIVE CHARACTERISTICS OF EMPLOYEES WHO EMBRACE COHESION

In Chapter 2, I introduced the seven attributes of leaders that make them effective at creating Cohesion Cultures. Now, I suggest there are three specific characteristics or behaviors found in employees who thrive in this type of culture. The first is the hunger for knowledge and information. The next behavior involves how employees relate to each through the concept of a collaborative conviction. The third characteristic reflects how the employee deals with change. Independent and distinct, these three characteristics provide a foundation for how the employee behaves within a Cohesion Culture for optimal success.

1. **Hunger for knowledge.** Leaders should look for people who want to learn. An employee who has a hunger for knowledge conveys, "I don't know everything, and I am open and willing to seek new information." Successful employees within a Cohesion Culture look to acquire information before the leader or supervisor tells them to do so. Just as being teachable is an important attribute for effective leaders of cohesion, it is important for employees, too. I like to think of the process as continual, satisfying, and useful. Being hungry for knowledge is not just about consuming until you can't take in anything else. It's about using what is learned to grow and develop. Employees who demonstrate this characteristic are eager to share what they are learning with peers, subordinates, and within all parts of the organization.

2. **Collaborative conviction.** In the realm of learning, when employees are collaborative, they agree everyone needs each other. No one person is better than the next, and employees adopt, hold on to, and foster this ideal at all times. It doesn't mean employees should be willing to say "yes" to everything. Seek employees who are contributors, add value, offer suggestions, challenge the status quo and are willing to build meaningful relationships with other individuals. Much like the leader, employees who have a collaborative approach to work build trust. Their actions reflect willingness to listen to the voice of others and consider its value before making final judgments of what to do next. This is essential to teamwork and reinforces the elements of belonging, value, and commitment within the Cohesion Culture.

3. **Change thinking.** How an employee approaches change can make or break the successful implementation of an organization's culture. Although change is often scary because

in many instances it deals with uncertainty, employees who pursue "change" through the lens of learning contribute to the growth and development of themselves and the organization. In other words, people who embrace change are individuals who think about the future. They understand the past, respect what they are doing in the present, but they look to the future knowing that it will take new information and a team of committed individuals to get there. Employees who embrace change also demonstrate open-mindedness and commitment to the best interest of others, even if it makes them feel slightly uncomfortable. Within change thinking, the employee actively leads the new process or improvement alongside the leader as an agent of change, not a barrier to the future.

## CHANGE THINKING FOR THE ORGANIZATION

Change thinking encourages open communication and dialogue within an organization. Once again, leaders are the agents of learning and change. In a learning organization, communication is open at all levels: top–down, side to side, and down–up. There must be organizational mechanisms—established processes—in place to allow information to move freely without fears of repercussion.

Years ago, when I worked for a company where the C-suite offices had walls of windows with blinds, in order to implement an "open-door, open-mind" philosophy—as an organizational mechanism—it was necessary that I also initiate an "open-blind" policy.

Leaders can also promote open communication and learn from their employees by conducting in-person interviews. During these sessions, the leader asks open-ended questions that allow the employee to provide valuable input and speak broadly on topics, as opposed to closed-ended questions that can stifle a more honest response. Open-ended questions provide leaders with understanding of individual perspectives.

Yet another mechanism leaders can implement to understand employee thinking is an employee survey. In anonymous surveys, employees can truly express how they feel and think, in their own words. The survey process automatically removes the need to make assumptions because behaviors are now defined by answers to the survey questions.

Overall, these organizational mechanisms allow the leader to gain a better understanding all around, far beyond the interpretation that comes through observation.

When leadership commits to embracing the components of a learning organization, it can't do so halfheartedly. All elements of a learning organization—generation, adaptability, experimentation, diversity, and stewardship—happen in tandem. For instance, if an organization only focused on experimentation, it wouldn't necessarily make an evaluation and thus wouldn't adapt, reshape, or innovate.

But wholeheartedly embracing change thinking as a learning organization means that you have access to an endless, self-generating supply of talent and information. Just as Mary's carpetbag was bottomless, containing whatever she needed for wherever she was at the time—be it a hat stand, a mirror, or a floor lamp—each employee contains immeasurable potential when a leader develops an individual relationship with him or her, and provides an open forum to learn and unlimited access to open communication with others. As these employees form a group or team, they replicate that behavior with each other—because, remember, everyone can be a leader by adopting the attributes of effective leadership. Leaders motivate, influence, and enable others to accomplish things otherwise impossible to do on one's own. This is why leaders should look at their employees just like Mary's carpetbag. As Mary wisely says, "Never judge things by their appearance—even carpetbags. I'm sure I never do."

## LESSONS LEARNED

- The double-loop mindset doesn't just correct a problem in the moment; it investigates the problem from a strategic standpoint, asking why the problem occurred and what the impact of possible changes will be in the future.
- Flattening the hierarchy of an organization creates cross-functional teams that improve an organization's productivity.
- Change thinking accepts learning as the basis for the way an organization does business.

# *Act 3:*
# *Talent Retention*
# *Comes to Life*

# CHAPTER 5

# *Retain Talent*

"If you want to go fast, go alone.
If you want to go far, go together."

**—African Proverb**

## KEY CONCEPTS:

1.12    *Synergy:* The way in which the combined action of all the parts creates a whole that is greater than the sum of the parts.

1.13    *Talent retention model:* A dynamic structure that provides the basis for a Cohesion Culture by supporting the overarching strategy of retaining talent.

1.14    *Learning:* The prong of the talent retention model concerned with gathering information, absorbing it, thinking about it, and testing its ability to stand up in an argument or debate.

1.15    *Relating:* Another prong of the talent retention model, concerned with how individuals use, exchange, and relate information with the goal of developing the best self in themselves and others.

The success of the organization lies in leadership, and most assuredly that includes the chief executive officer. Success starts with the CEO, and this is especially true of my experience at South Carolina Federal. With a single comment during a presentation, a CEO can shift the entire culture of the organization. Even the smallest action has an impact. For this reason, creating and sustaining a Cohesion Culture requires that leaders know "parts are parts" so they can communicate this to their followers. This is not just a catchphrase to minimize the individual and collective pieces of a whole concept, idea, or item. It recognizes that all the parts matter and how they work together truly reflects the opportunity for success or the consequences of failure. While we are able to describe them in and of themselves and see them as distinct, their value lies in working together.

In this regard, being a learning organization is an outcome of synergy, where the total of all of the parts is greater than the sum of them individually. I truly believe we are not as successful individually as we are when we work collectively toward a common and shared goal. That's where cohesion lives—in the collective work, the collaborative mind, and the actions that make the most sense because they are the right things to do.

When leadership uses core values, beliefs, attitudes, and behaviors to guide conversations of autonomy, initiative, and character, then the culture shifts from a transactional one to one that supports cohesion. The talent retention model works at its best when management has built a value system around honesty, accountability, teamwork, professionalism, shared vision, and positive attitude, and when those core values lead to shared beliefs, attitudes, and behaviors of those who work in the organization. When this happens, the following are true:

1. The organization operates from an authentic and honest position to maintain a people-centric mission.
2. Senior leadership supports the culture in word and deed. This means that leaders examine their mindset and seek the voice of others to promote action that models best-

self behavior and inspires employees to do the same. It means that leadership is actively engaged in promoting a learning organization. It has adopted the seven values of leadership that encourage cohesion: being teachable, having compassion, extending grace, seeking truth, showing humility, exhibiting a pure heart, and bringing peace.

3. The culture is so well-defined as such that all employees can live it, breathe it and own it. People feel they belong. People understand their purpose, do meaningful work, and understand theirs and others' value. They commit to the shared and desired outcomes that serve self and the organization.

Once these transformative behaviors are fully engaged, then the Cohesion Culture emerges.

In the nearly fourteen years since I started at South Carolina Federal Credit Union, we have stayed the course to be an "Employer of Choice." We wanted our employees to feel special about working at the organization. Our HR strategies and practices centered on becoming one of the Best Places to Work. Why? When people love where they work, take care of each other and have a desire to grow and learn, magic happens. The parts become so much more. And the winners are always people: the employees, the consumers, the community. "Parts are parts" means nothing if they are not implemented simultaneously; each part is successful based on the success of others. Below, I introduce the *talent retention model* as the basis for supporting a "parts are parts" mentality.

## TALENT RETENTION MODEL

The talent retention model (TRM) is the basis for a Cohesion Culture. It is a dynamic structure whose purpose is to support the overarching strategy of retaining talent, which should be the number-one objective of all businesses, followed by consistently increasing revenue. In reality, these are not separate objectives. When transformative leaders shift the focus away from talent acquisition and toward investing in and developing a cohesive team, the path to increased revenue becomes straighter and easier.

The TRM embodies four concepts, outlined below, that support the three relational aspects of the employee journey—sense of belonging, employee value, and commitment to goals. This model reinforces the core values and beliefs of any organization. Identifying these key pieces creates an environment where employees have a sense of belonging and value, which leads them to make a full commitment to the organization.

## THE FOUR CONCEPTS

1.   Emotional and Spiritual Growth

This may seem like an odd place to start, but it's not accidental that it comes first in the TRM. I firmly believe that we are, as individuals, far more than the sum of our parts. What makes us individuals is our yearning for purpose, for meaning, for connection with something higher and greater than ourselves.

Companies who acknowledge this are really only acknowledging the obvious, which to deny is fatuous and counterproductive. And yet, it's clear that companies are *afraid* to address this aspect of people that turns them from unthinking structures and processes into living, breathing entities. But they needn't be. Once this deep-seated need for meaningful purpose is both addressed and aligned with the organization's mission, a flood of passion is unleashed that can accomplish truly great, even transcendent things. And if you're still wondering why we need passion in the workplace, remember, passion is what people experience when they are doing what they know is important and has value.

## 2.   Physical and Mental Well-Being

Here I want to again return to Maslow's hierarchy of needs, one of the pillars of behavioral motivation. Basic needs of survival and safety must be met before there is energy or motivation for any higher achievements of intellect or creativity. While your employees may not be starving or afraid for their lives, if they are physically unwell and mentally stressed at work, productivity plummets.

This may sound mercenary, but it is simply a fact. We should care about our employees' well-being because they are valuable as people, but it also makes good business sense to care, and to put programs in place to support mental and physical health by encouraging healthy practices both in and out of the workplace, and by providing an environment in which those practices can realistically take place. This kind of support creates employee satisfaction and behaviors consistent with cohesion.

## 3.   Financial Mindset

Financial security is part of the basic need for safety. Financial *independence* is a primary aspect of retention success. An organization's role in supporting its employees' financial health involves much more than offering a competitive paycheck, good health care and retirement benefits, and monetary bonuses. It requires teaching money management skills in the areas of savings mobilization and credit utilization, and in such a way that promotes financial learning as a positive behavior and not just corrective action.

Financial stress is also an aspect of mental health; when employees are stressed about money or living paycheck to paycheck, which can happen at any income level, they are less able to perform at an optimal level. So, once again, investing in employees in this area enables them to invest more and more fully in their contributions to the organization.

4.  Intellectual Stimuli

In today's workforce, it is impossible to separate intellectual stimulation from the development of an entrepreneurial spirit. Even within the framework of an organizational structure, employees desire autonomy and a collaborative work environment where they are asked to think and encouraged to contribute. They want to think for themselves, solve problems, and be creative. In short, they want to be treated like adults, not children who have to be supervised and told how to think.

In addition to educational and skill-developing programs, the open exchange of ideas in a team-building environment is a key part of intellectual stimulation. As team members see that they can inspire colleagues and even management with valuable input, they learn that everyone can be a leader. An organization that challenges employees' intellects also signals to them that they are valued and that they belong.

You'll notice that each of these four concepts addresses a need all people have in their personal lives as well. The overlap between personal and work life cannot be underestimated if talent is to be retained. Employees are looking for quality of life in the office as well as at home, and these four elements should ideally be implemented seamlessly across both spaces.

HR is where the rubber meets the road in implementing the four concepts of the TRM so that they become a foundation for organization culture and an embodiment of organizational values. When it comes to retaining talent, CEOs can't do their job effectively if the strategies and practices of the HR department aren't solid. When HR implements these structures so that the talent is truly connected within the organization, a Cohesion Culture is created.

At South Carolina Federal Credit Union, the HR voice is strong under the direction of Leslie Norris, senior VP of Human Resources & Development. Leslie has a seat at the management table right alongside Finance, Retail Sales, Lending, Marketing, Operations, Audit, and Information Technology. The strategies from all of our business units is reflected in the corporate business plan, which is available for our entire staff to read and adopt, not just for the board, senior management, and key leaders.

## COHESION

*Cohesion positively impacts performance in all stages of a group's development.* This was the hypothesis of my dissertation for the research that brought the talent retention model to life. As I have stated previously, cohesion directly produces increased performance.

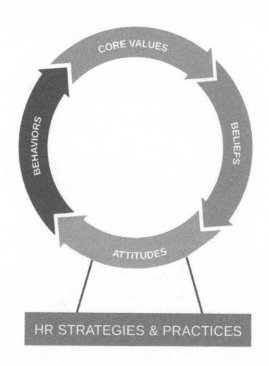

Cohesion Culture is a people-centric strategy that starts with core values. Once these core values are defined with specific guiding principles that reflect the characteristics of the business, this value system must be integrated within every aspect of key HR practices such as acquisition, compensation and benefits, well-being initiatives, performance and coaching, and development. How does management do this? By modeling learning organization behavior, cultivating a transformational leadership mindset and inspiring aspirational vision.

1. **Model behavior consistent with a learning organization.** Generation, adaptability, experimentation, diversity, and stewardship—these behaviors create safe spaces to experiment, make mistakes, and learn from failure. They encourage us to explore our fears of change and learn from them so that we can grow into change thinking.

2. **Cultivate a transformational leadership mindset.** If your leadership simply focuses on goals, primarily those around the concept of a concrete product, you are likely leaning towards a transactional mindset, which means that the company's processes only solve for today and not necessarily for tomorrow. If this describes your company, you should consider making a cultural adjustment to a transformational model of leadership that focuses on aligning values and making changes with the future in mind. Otherwise it will be impossible to create an atmosphere of trust, value, and belonging that is essential to having a cohesive effect on increasing performance.

3. **Inspire aspirational vision.** While inspiring someone by focusing on the outcome is a transactional form of leadership, setting employees on the path of aspiring toward a vision of hope for the future signifies a transformational mindset. In the beginning, this was a difficult concept for our staff at the credit union. We excelled at being reactive to what the consumer needed. Staff was friendly and helpful because it impacted the present, not the future. All the attention to setting sales

goals and numbers was born of a sales culture. This was an epic fail. Performance evaluations were myopically geared to report and measure one's ability to hit a target. Although the primary mission of the credit union is to improve the financial condition of peoples' lives, we missed the opportunity to help them in the future because we failed to help them identify their own needs for the future.

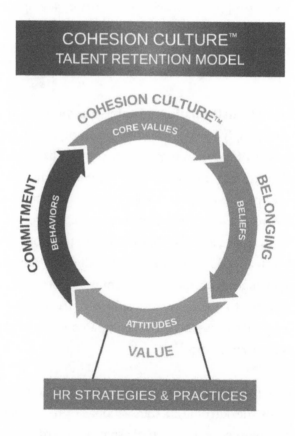

Only when leaders start with a focus on the development of others can the transformation toward a Cohesion Culture occur.. And when they understand their own purpose and value as a part of the organization, they commit to achieving the desired outcomes of the organization.

Instead, our focus was directed at measurable, immediate targets and not the value of people. I am not suggesting numbers aren't important. On the contrary, goals create guidelines, and guidelines direct activity with the intent of bringing order to what would be chaos. But they cannot be the primary focus of the organization. Instead, today our model is to coach toward values-based performance as defined by the cornerstone ideals of the organization.

## LEARNING AND RELATING: A TWO-PRONGED APPROACH

Once the four concepts of the TRM are in place, the next steps are to implement the key pieces of learning and relating.

## LEARNING

Learning is the part of the model responsible for gathering information, absorbing it, thinking about it, and testing its ability to stand up in an argument or debate. It's what the employee learns that can be put to use. This process is circular and allows for the continual development of staff, meaning that individuals who are learning are in a constant state of acquiring new information. Once they have determined its value, either discarded or absorbed, they are ready to replicate the process. Though I explain this in a linear fashion, the process is dynamic. Our brains process information at a very quick rate and make determinations about its relevance and then repeat the process. This is exactly how you are interacting with the information in this book. You are trying to make sense of the new information, evaluating it based on what you may already know and hopefully on where you want to take your employees and the organization.

I think of the learning process as though all the information you receive is water. Operating on a continuum from sponge to rock, people need to decide where to be. Sponge or rock? Generally, most people want to be a sponge and soak up all the information they can because they know information is powerful and can help them make well-informed decisions. However, there is nothing wrong with being a rock. Sometimes we come in contact with information that is simply not beneficial, and it is my advice that you let it roll off you, exactly how water interacts with a rock. Throughout the learning process, people often reflect many stages of acceptance on the "sponge to rock" scale.

Part of the learning process must include experimentation, one of the primary tenets of the learning organization. The environment in which individuals operate must be safe. There must be room for error. Leaders are encouraged to foster an environment for individuals to be honest even when they make mistakes. If those mistakes aren't forgiven, the learning ability and growth of both the individual and the organization will be greatly diminished. When learning is suppressed or halted, people cannot move forward. To sum up how I feel about learning, "You don't have to know everything; you just need to be teachable."

The learning prong has three main components:

1.  **Observation.** People learn in a variety of ways. Observation plays the largest role in a Cohesion Culture because people are more likely to imitate what they observe versus what they read or hear. The old adage rings true: "A picture is worth a thousand words." As an individual experiences and learns firsthand, they take into account three elements: they evaluate what they hear, touch and see within a scale of personal assessment and congruency. This is why building effective leaders and putting the right culture in place is necessary. People who are committed to learning will seek new information from both written and auditory sources. The greatest impact comes from what the individual observes. They will ask, "Does this make sense to me? Is it valuable? Can I adopt these actions for my own?" If the

answers are affirmative, individuals are more likely to take
that information and think of ways to adopt it.

2.  **Imitation.** As individuals make sense of their observations,
    they experiment by imitating. It is a form of testing the waters
    to see how it feels and how others will react. A leader must
    ensure his behavior is worthy of being imitated by those who
    see it. When people imitate or experiment, they develop a
    level of comfort and make the new action their own. Once the
    individual is comfortable with the new behavior, it becomes
    part of them. This is how people take ownership of what
    they have learned.

3.  **Mindset.** Throughout this book, there has been considerable
    information on establishing the mindset of the leader.
    Considering the mindset of all the people within the culture
    is necessary to ensure cohesion. As the leader focuses on the
    five mindsets presented in Chapter 2, the employee's mindset
    or attitude toward learning should be one of accepting change
    as part of ongoing development and advancement. How the
    individual thinks about information, its value, importance,
    and relevance will shape how quickly the Cohesion Culture
    comes into place. And it will contribute to how effective
    leaders are at keeping it in place.

To support the learning prong of the talent retention model,
South Carolina Federal has a learning and teaching online university
program. This robust onsite learning platform includes computer-
based training systems as well as classroom training and is
supplemented from outside the four walls of the organization with
certifications and partnership studies at technical schools, colleges,
and universities.

## THE SIXTEEN-MILLION-DOLLAR LAB

Experimentation is part of learning—a process to try new ideas without the fear of failure. Experimentation is generally best when those conducting experiments are cautious—not cautious to avoid mistakes, but cautious to avoid blowing up a laboratory.

Jack Welch, former CEO of General Electric, and his wife, Suzy, wrote the book *Winning* in 2001. In the section dedicated to experimentation, Welch writes that as a young leader, he was responsible for a sixteen-million-dollar lab that blew up! When he was called into the CEO's office, he assumed he'd immediately be fired, so he rehearsed his resignation. The best he could hope for was to leave the company on his own terms. As Jack fumbled through his speech, the CEO cocked his head and asked, "Jack, what are you talking about?" Sheepishly, Jack offered, "I thought you were going to fire me because I blew up the lab, and I was trying to find a way to resign." Sternly the CEO responded, "Are you kidding me? I just paid sixteen million dollars to train you. I'm not about to let you go now."

Clearly, getting a little soot on your nose the first time you clean a chimney is a lot different than losing sixteen million dollars. All the same, it is important that the leader and the organization have an experimental approach to finding innovative solutions that meet the needs of the talent.

Although most companies could not sustain that type of loss, it was clear the CEO understood the value of experimentation and its impact on learning. It is through learning that individuals move toward aspirations of growth and development. Learning is the foundation for the second prong, relating.

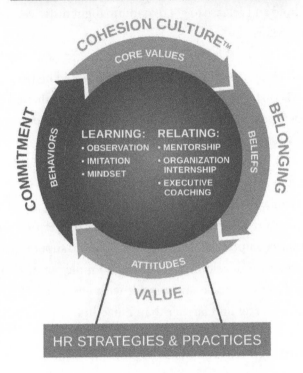

## RELATING

In my early childhood, my younger brother and I would challenge each other to fly paper airplanes. We began by making the traditional, aerodynamic versions. You know—the ones with the sleek bodies and pointed tips. Standing behind the broomstick starting line at the beginning of the hallway, each flight challenge began. The goal was to see whose plane would fly the farthest and stay in the air the longest. I'd like to think that my superior aviation skills contributed to my success. Alas, I doubt it. More than likely, it was our age difference.

My winning streak continued until one day my brother asked for help. With the motivated coaching from mom, my reluctance diminished, and soon we had created the Hall Brothers Paper Airplane Flight School. I taught him how to carefully fold and press down the creases until he had built the perfect aircraft. We practiced the art of hold and release to get maximum flight distance. He passed with flying colors.

I would love to think I fit the perfect role of sage, teacher and coach in all instances with my brother. That would be fiction. What I do know is that the power of relationship is strengthened through the quality time and effort we invest in others. It's for their sake, not ours that we should do this right thing and offer advice, instruction and feedback, so they can fly. Time has gone by. I am all grown up. Unfortunately, my flying paper aircraft days are over. Or are they? Metaphorically, I've been tossing paper planes in the air all my life.

In the context of the talent retention model, the relating prong has three primary components with each designed to support a different level of employee development. Through employee development, leaders fold, mold, crease and release with every intent of having their plane go faster and farther than it had boldly gone before.

1.  **Mentoring.** Mentoring is a relationship-building activity between two professionals that allows for an exchange of information for the purpose of development, advancement, or succession. In a mentoring program there is a mentee—a young professional—and a mentor—a seasoned or experienced leader.

2.  **Organizational internship.** This kind of internship is differentiated from a traditional internship because it provides opportunities for employees already within the organization to become familiar with different departments and roles within the company, providing insight into future possibilities for advancement.

3.  **Executive coaching.** Executive coaching is career-focused rather than job-focused and involves developing the skills and strengths to succeed in an upper management or senior role.

Each of these programs supports various stages of an employee's development and advancement within the organization.

## COMPONENT #1: MENTORING

Mentoring is first on the relating prong because in a transformative leadership model that supports Cohesion Culture, a leader focuses on the outcomes of the individual first and then on organizational success.

Mentoring builds from the information an employee already has or the knowledge he is acquiring through social learning, reading, listening or doing. A successful mentoring program should be structured in a way that encourages the mentee to challenge the status quo, rip the information apart and dissect it for greater value. It establishes a safe place in which individuals can discuss complex topics and create practical ways to use the knowledge in the mentee's continued development. Sometimes the mentee wants to know how to handle his or her boss. Having a safe place to ask questions that may seem accusatory or limited in perspective is extremely helpful to long-term success for the mentee.

This type of mentoring includes collaboration and trust. Collaboration occurs when both individuals engaged in the process agree they need each other. Both must have an equal voice and be teachable. Having trust in a relationship gives it substance and offers a strong foundation for removing any dysfunctions, such as unhealthy conflict, lack of accountability, stifled communication, and inattention to results.

The mentee and mentor roles are defined such that the mentee expresses a personal goal or development opportunity and the mentor helps the mentee achieve it. As this relates to the talent retention model within an organization that is developing a culture of cohesion, that individual activity must align with an organizational outcome. Otherwise, the fruits of the mentoring activity would be less productive as part of the Cohesion Culture.

The mentee and mentor relationship can occur between an employee and a supervisor as well as between individuals from different companies. The role of the mentor is to invest, encourage, and guide the individual mentee to their mutual and desired outcomes. Goal clarity is extremely important to this process.

## THE GLOBAL IMPACT OF MENTORING

Sometimes the mentee and the mentor relationship is cross-generational or multicultural, which in today's global economy brings about many benefits.

While in the Philippines in 2018, I had the pleasure of working with Konstantin Comeros, area director for credit union development at VICTO National. Our work together inspired us to create the Global Leadership Exchange (GLE) Program, which in its inaugural year brought together two leaders from different countries for a fifteen-day cultural-immersion event.

The primary focus of the GLE Program is to facilitate the transfer of knowledge specific to cultural diversity and inclusion as it relates to talent retention. In addition to the traditional mentoring activities, the two participants met with local HR professionals, corporate business leaders, social activists, and community leadership to discuss real, not theoretical, talent retention issues facing these groups today.

This is the type of action that a Cohesion Culture brings forth. A Cohesion Culture naturally promotes creative innovation through the individual and collective works of others.

The GLE Program is supported by the Credit Union Development Education Program (CUDE). Also, South Carolina State House

Representatives Joe Daning (District 92) and Nancy Mace (District 99) sponsored a House resolution bringing statewide attention to the work of the GLE for credit unions here in the United States and around the globe. The resolution recognized the program and our efforts to support the cooperative financial model with specific attention to leadership development in the areas of cultural diversity and inclusion, and talent retention.

## EMPLOYEE DEVELOPMENT

At South Carolina Federal Credit Union, we offer a three-year management development program aimed at guiding individuals who are considered high-potential employees (HPE) to future success. The organizational leaders choose employees who have the potential to serve in a supervisory or leadership capacity within various areas of the organization.

The curriculum starts by focusing on personal development during year one. Employees learn the core leadership values, the concepts of influence thinking and how to apply them, how to distinguish between leadership styles, and the difference between transactional and transformational behaviors.

In year two, employees begin the journey of developing others within the organization. They continue to receive coaching and guidance where their performance-management skills are developed and refined. And they may participate in an organizational internship program (described later in detail).

In year three, participants have the opportunity to then develop outside the organization, within the industry and the community. They have opportunities to network with peers and colleagues within industry-specific conferences and events and are also encouraged to become part of a community cause, serving on a board or committee or as a volunteer.

The CUaware Mentoring program was a collaborative effort between myself and Will Crosswell, who ran business development for Palmetto Citizens Federal Credit Union in Columbia, South Carolina. Before the formation of the Carolinas Credit Union League that incorporated both North and South Carolina trade associations, Will and I discovered a missed opportunity in the development of young professionals who chose a career in the credit union industry and, more importantly, wanted to stay. Succession planning and development was a weakness in credit unions and most organizations.

During the pilot phase of the program, we documented the process, revamped it, and helped the league implement the program in both North and South Carolina. What started in 2012 with two participants has grown to impact hundreds of young and seasoned professionals.

A shorter version is an eleven-month program designed to function around six to eight required meetings (virtual or physical), a shadowing event where the mentee visits the mentor's credit union and vice versa, and a 250-word essay expressing the benefits of the program. It is supported by monthly check-ins and quarterly online trainings where panel discussions happen virtually and in physical classroom settings.

## COMPONENT #2: ORGANIZATIONAL INTERNSHIP

The second aspect of the relating prong deals with organizational internship. Not to be confused with the traditional type of internship that provides learning opportunities for external candidates, this program is internal. As the organization builds momentum in forming a Cohesion Culture, an organizational internship program provides an opportunity for individuals to put their knowledge to use.

Organizational internships work in tandem with mentoring. A well-known best practice is for interns to take what they have learned from the acquisition or transfer-of-knowledge activities and meld it with their mentoring experience through a hands-on activity. Mentoring provides the opportunity to discuss and examine what is being learned, while an organizational internship provides the opportunity to put what is learned into action.

Career services counseling is one specific HR practice necessary to support an organizational internship initiative. The career coach meets with individuals throughout the organization and helps them define how they can best be used in a meaningful role. As we've discussed, people want to have purpose and do work that is meaningful and important. This purpose or drive helps them navigate their specific development plan. The career coach has a macro view of the organization and, in cohesive leadership form, works for the success of both the individual and the company. These career coaches are like the yentas of corporate matchmaking, except there is no dating, just a marriage between employee and organization. Through a career-services approach that balances past, present, and future, the intended outcome is to provide an independent look at the potential for a career track for employees who want to advance within the organization. Again, the model supports the aspect of commitment within the Cohesion Culture. It is transformative as well. The development plan first focuses on others, then the organization. When this alignment occurs, employees see how they are considered to be a part of the parts with the intent to belong, be valued, and commit to outcomes of success for all.

At South Carolina Federal, two different types of organizational internship have been created to support the culture of cohesion: 1) traditional cross-training from one department to another, and 2) role reversal within the same department. These examples are just two ways an organization can innovate and save their talent from exiting the back door as quickly as they entered the front.

In the traditional cross-training program, individuals may work in other departments to see if they have greater value there. Of greatest value for employees is that should a future need arise, they can respond to the internal posting and leverage the documented organizational internship program. This is a tremendous benefit to the individual and the organization. Internal talent is retained and better aligned to its purpose. The cost savings to the organization averages about 25 percent of a person's salary. An employee making $60,000 who leaves costs the organization $15,000 to retrain a new recruit. This does not include the monies spent on acquisition, nor does it account for the opportunity cost associated with the organizational intelligence taken with the exiting staff.

Through the role-reversal option, an individual serving as the department supervisor assumes a temporary junior role. De facto, the supervisor relinquishes appropriate authority to a department intern who will perform as supervisor throughout the internship period, albeit under the care of the aforementioned supervisor. This gives a junior associate an opportunity to test-drive a managerial role—just like test-driving a car before buying it. And the added benefit is the supervisor now has an idea how that employee drives. Internships are just another way for leaders to exercise learning through experimentation that is safe and at a minimal cost. No lab explosion necessary.

Organizational internships are both practical and necessary. If organizations do not provide for them, they risk losing the talent to another organization that offers that same type of job or allows that employee the opportunity to fulfill their purpose or meaning. It is less costly for the organization to retain employees and move them to other departments and roles within an organization than to leave them where they are until they became so unproductive and disconnected that they choose to leave. Both mentorship and organizational internships create greater opportunity of development for individuals still finding their way to the top.

## COMPONENT # 3: EXECUTIVE COACHING

The third element of the talent retention model's relating prong is executive coaching, which appeals to individuals at a senior level either by position or by tenure. It is an opportunity for them to move to a higher realm of self-actualization and in turn self-management. Executive coaching is closely tied to succession development in our organization. Succession development, as the name implies, is geared toward employees identified as candidates who could possibly move into higher levels of supervision and management when an opening occurs.

This level of coaching deals intimately with curating the strengths that are needed for someone to accomplish a "next level" job, or to be more proficient in their existing upper-management or senior role. Executive coaching must inspire an aspirational mindset directing employees to think more about the career they want than the job they have. This is important to the concept of "I am." Through coaching on an executive level, individuals must declare their leadership competence now and in the present.

This opportunity for development is not intended to fix something or to be overly complex in its intended outcome. In organizations that do not have a Cohesion Culture mindset, executive coaching can be seen as a last-ditch effort to save executives. In subsequent discussions I have learned that a participant's mind and actions were on the surface agreeable. But on the inside the thoughts were focused on "What's wrong with me," or the "Someday I will be good enough" syndrome.

However, in organizations that drive to create a culture of cohesion, this same program is positively viewed as a win-win. It's a combination of mentoring and internship focused on the continued development of individuals with senior-level authority and widespread corporate responsibility. If organizations view executive coaching as corrective, then they should consider investing their resources elsewhere.

Looking tactically at mentorship, organizational internship, and executive coaching, an organization can appeal to the learning and development needs for all levels of employees within their culture. Employees deserve to have in place specific tactics that allow and provide for their development. It sends a clear signal that all employees matter; they are not just another resource, like raw materials, to produce an outcome. Instead, they are contributing forces in the success of the organization because they are providing meaningful work, accomplishing tasks, and acting to achieve desired outcomes.

When leaders engage the talent retention model on an individual and collective level, they acknowledge that parts are parts. These activities within the model support cohesion by engendering a sense of belonging, establishing value, and gaining commitment. Having a talent retention model in place provides greater opportunities for individuals to be retained because they have a path of development.

## BACKLIGHT BLUE

Two of my very favorite and career-rewarding experiences include working with the CEO of South Carolina Federal Credit Union, Scott Woods, and the credit union's senior VP of human resources, Leslie Norris. Scott provides the needed leadership and support to nurture and grow the culture through cohesion activities by empowering senior management to be advocates for the employees. Leslie is the person I fondly call the "Champion of People and Culture." We have partnered to create many of the programs introduced at the credit union that are reflected within the talent retention model.

In 2006, Leslie and I began working on making sense of the company's core values and how they impacted the behaviors of the talent. We started by studying successful cultures like Starbucks, Disney and the Pike Street Fish Market. We researched and read many books about the companies' inner workings, which gave us insight into their successful cultures. But it wasn't until we revisited our experiences with the Pike Street Fish Market in Seattle, Washington, and saw it in action, that a plan for our own company came together.

We started by researching how the Seattle-based coffee company Starbucks turned buying java into a fad and made their street-corner coffee shops a destination. With the proliferation of the coffee shop, literally one on every corner, we did not need to travel too far for observation. Starbucks created an internal culture rich with employee-centric opportunities. Each barista was encouraged to have an entrepreneurial mindset and to connect with people on a social basis. Leadership created the concept of what it would be like every time a Starbucks employee donned the green apron. To some degree, the green apron was like an employee costume.

From there, our minds raced to Disney and what we knew from personal experience. Every Disney character has a costume, and with that costume comes very specific ways a character interacts with other park members and guests at the park. Once employees put on their costumes, they are required to act like the character regardless of where they roam. It does not matter if Snow White walks the cobblestone streets around the castle or takes a break behind the gates. If she wears the costume, she acts like the character. Disney is very serious about this and has been known to fire employees who let their guard down in a location the patrons may consider "backstage." For Disney, there is only "stage"—no front and no back. Wear the costume, act the part.

Although our visits to the Pike Street Fish Market were separate, they were extremely powerful in setting a foundation for our company culture. We came back with very similar feelings about the need to create a work environment that allowed people to be part of something fun and to see value in what they did. In the market, we observed people who were mainly just buying fish, taking it home for the evening's entrée or having it shipped somewhere around the world. But the workers were engaged in one of the most physically challenging lines of work and they were having fun! They shared the fun with people passing by and the willing-to-participate customers.

It was an everyday, early-to-rise job that seemed more like an arcade or amusement park than a for-profit business. Part of the interest and what attracted so much attention was how employees delivered the fish from one person to the next after it had been selected. They threw it to each other with flair; the fish-throwing was an art form. Although it had been done a thousand times before, every time someone caught a fish, they celebrated like it was the first time. We saw firsthand how leaders in the fish market involved employees and customers in the cultural experience.

I merely observed. Leslie, on the other hand, is an "in the moment" kinda person. She became part of the experience without much prodding or encouragement. Leslie even has video that clearly shows the exuberance and excitement that builds from people being included and valued. One of the employees invited her behind the counter. At first, she thought this was great. Then her eyes glazed over in momentary shock. They did not want her to just observe— she was going to make the next big catch!

In order to keep up the appearance of confidence, Leslie became a learner—a social learner—and a quick one at that. To be successful she would need to take what she observed, imitate the behavior, and then implement it to complete the task at hand.

Leslie held out her arms as instructed. One of the good-natured employees stood behind her to let her know he would catch it if she missed. On the count of three they would throw the fish. One, two, throw. Yes, you guessed it, they threw after two. But Leslie was ready. You should have seen her eyes light up when she caught that fish. The applause from other customers was instantaneous and genuine.

This experience showed us exactly what it's like when employees in a work environment feel like a team and like they're part of something special. The way they interacted could not have been staged. In both of our visits, we interviewed staff, and it quickly became apparent how much their bosses cared for them, found ways to rotate employees' daily tasks to avoid job burnout, and taught them how to extend what they were doing beyond the walls of the market into the street. Those leaders took what might have been a mundane job and made it have value. It was perfect for what we wanted to do.

So, between catching fish, wearing a green apron, and donning a Disney character costume, we knew the most obvious way to connect how people behaved based on core values was to establish our own standards. The task was daunting. As a credit union, we are a not-for-profit financial cooperative, and although we earn money from activities, our profits are invested with our members. How in the world would we be able to take this concept born from a for-profit model and make it our own?

## THE EPIPHANY

One day, after staring at numerous white flip-chart papers taped to the wall, we realized what needed to happen. We asked ourselves, "Why were these activities of throwing fish and serving coffee and acting like a cartoon character successful?" Our answer was not a *what* but a *who*. We came to understand that these activities had nothing to do with money. They had everything to do with the character of the people performing the activities, and how they acted toward others. The sense of comradery at the market was not from catching and packaging fish; it came from how they treated each other. Starbucks and Disney simply gave people structure on how to behave and how to ensure guests' experiences would keep them coming back.

At that moment, whether we knew what to call it or not, we wanted to create an environment where people thrived and wanted to stay. We wanted to bring respect and honor to the task of taking care of people, especially their financial well-being, and to focus on developing people for the future—theirs and ours. Only with a true collaboration could we have succeeded in creating a culture of cohesion. Instead of finding out what employees didn't like about our company, we set the expectation of becoming one of the Best Places to Work. Our quest began.

The task at hand turned to core values. Were they the right ones? What practices did we have that supported employees? We knew that core values establish the foundation for beliefs, and attitudes are a result of how we express those beliefs; when we combine core values, beliefs, and attitudes, we get behaviors. We decided to start there.

We reevaluated our core values and defined them as *honesty, accountability, teamwork, share the vision, professionalism,* and *positive attitude.* It is easy to see how these values morphed from our experiences and the rich eighty-plus-year history of the credit union. Everything we wanted was wrapped up into those six values. (On a side note, technically *positive attitude* is an outcome of values and beliefs, but we felt so strongly that our environment had to have positive thinking that we did not leave it up to chance.)

During our working session, we decided to keep the list of behaviors small and manageable. We knew from previous leadership best practices that focusing on big items and a small list would make these behaviors easy to learn, simple to train, and effortless to carry out on a daily basis. Finally, in order to create a visual for these behaviors, and inspired by the words *green apron,* we thought about what color could work for us. Blue was the primary color used in all our branding materials, so we decided, why fight it? Blue it was.

Leslie and I created BLUE behaviors:

- Bright
- Listener
- Understanding
- Energetic

*Bright* describes how employees welcome and greet one another and our clients. It's how we respond to another person, whether you see them for the first time or every day. We encourage greeting everyone you see in the hallways and to create a sense of connection and have meaningful encounters that express care and concern. This should happen at desks, in the hallways, transitioning from workspace to meeting room, or just enjoying downtime in the common area during a break. Greetings break the ice and through repeated interaction help define the way everyone should be treated.

*Listener* demonstrates that people matter. Listening promotes empathy and compassion. When a person listens and then responds to someone, they demonstrate that what that person says matters. When we listen, we gain information and insight. When others feel listened to, they are more willing to open up and share what they really think and who they really are.

*Understanding* is used by the one listening to reflect back what is heard. It's an opportunity for the listener to express and demonstrate empathy—the emotional path between you and another person. When we express empathy and understanding, we show the other person we care, and that can provide a sense of belonging. We encourage the talent to imagine what it might be like to walk in another person's shoes.

Rounding out BLUE is *Energetic*. This is vital. Energy is where relationships ignite and magic happens. We encourage energy that's positive and noticeable and creates a "wow" experience because energy begets energy. And when it comes to human connection, two positives always spark a positive sum.

We formed BLUE to give structure to how we wanted our core values, beliefs, and attitudes to manifest. It was a perfect match with our branding elements, and we created what stands today as the four main behaviors every one of our employees needs to know. Through our onboarding, coaching, and training programs, employees are reminded that the way to success is to bleed BLUE. If they act in this way that totally supports our core values and beliefs, they will have a healthy and happy life working here.

Every one of our employees now goes through a Dr. Troy leadership session to complete their first week of the onboarding experience. During the session, we reinforce that everyone is a leader. That means acting BLUE by leading and coaching to core values. We do not leave it to chance that employees will understand and adopt fundamental customs, rituals, traditions, and symbols that express who we are. We honestly communicate that if BLUE culture is not right for them, they can turn over their name badge during the break and leave. No harm. No foul. Everyone selected—not hired, but handpicked—to work here demonstrates a tremendous amount of positive attitude and alignment to organizational values. If they fake a positive attitude to get hired, they're going to need to keep faking it to stay employed.

We also wanted to embody BLUE in a tangible, memorable way. We wanted to make sure the behaviors were tied into the costume, so to speak. After several weeks of deliberation, we settled on all employees wearing the same color top: our corporate blue. We shared this information with senior management to nods of agreement. Then one of our colleagues touched a nerve by saying, "So, we're going to make everyone wear logowear." I thought Leslie was going to fly out of her seat like she had just been ejected from a fighter jet in *Top Gun*. Leslie is passionate about the culture; she is what I call the very first of our Culture Keepers™. She informed the team it was not logowear. It was *brandwear*. *We* are the brand. Everything we say and do reflects upon the people of this organization.

Establishing a color code within the culture helped heighten a sense of belonging. It creates value because every individual, from the senior-most person in the organization to a new recruit, wears blue. Of course, there are a few exceptions. On occasions we have a business meeting, and the expectations of the attire may require a dress or suit and tie. But blue is our green apron or Disney costume, and it clearly reminds us all how we should behave or respond to others within the organization and to others outside the organization when we are wearing blue. It is amazing how this one little decision has had positive results in so many different areas. BLUE created the community of belonging and value.

Also, when we are out of the office and in the community, we provide employees with T-shirts appropriately sized and styled for all body types. Wearing the blue in public has produced an interesting byproduct. Waitstaff at restaurants recognize the color and often want to sit all of us together even when we accidentally show up at the same restaurant. Also, our members find it easier to tell who can help them when they enter our financial centers. We employ an open concept, and many of our folks freely roam throughout the space helping people at desks, while seated, and even while they are in line.

We do have a few cautionary advisements. For instance, if employees choose to drive aggressively to work, we suggest they put on their blue when they arrive in the parking lot. Why? Because I have gotten phone calls about the driving styles of our employees from people who knew they worked for our credit union because of the blue shirt. This is Disney at its best. When you put it on, act like what it means, or don't wear it until you do. Everyone is on the team; there are no back or front stages. There is only "on stage." These standards are in place and remain there because they speak to how we think and act, and in addition to living, breathing and owning it, we can now all *wear* it.

I am not kidding when I say if you don't have the rigor to put these types of policies in place, you are wasting your time trying to get the team-performance result. If you think that just reading this book, giving it to your training staff to develop a program, and then offering a course means you have put the framework of a culture together, you've misunderstood what I've communicated. If it sounds like you have to drink the Kool-Aid to work here, then so be it. In fact, I am so passionate about our concept of BLUE, I want people who will manufacture the ingredients, make the mixture, serve it up, and drink it, too. I want the Kool-Aid as long as it is the appropriate color BLUE.

## SOUNDCHECK FOR COHESION

> "If the top performer is making everyone miserable,
> fire them. You have to be in line with culture."
>
> **—Gary Vaynerchuck, best-selling author,**
> **founder of VaynerMedia & Speaker**

The surest way to tell whether or not an organization's culture is cohesive is by walking the halls of your organization on any given day. It doesn't take a degree in social behavior to recognize what's going on; it just takes a soundcheck. Describe the atmosphere. What do you see? What do you hear? What's the vibe? Listen especially to the sounds. How your culture sounds tells you a lot about what sort of culture you've built. Listen for greetings and laughter, signs that people are happy, comfortable, at home. Silence is your sonic boom. If you don't hear anything, there's a problem. While you surely don't want some raucous workplace where no one can get anything done, if it's too quiet, things are amiss. Trust me on this. It's a little like leaving a classroom of three-year-olds alone; if you don't hear a peep, trouble is probably brewing.

As part of my 2017 College of Charleston international MBA program visit to Duke Manufacturing in Prague, we discussed the similarities and differences in employee culture between the United States and the Czech Republic. One of the conversations uncovered how important it is for employees to feel included and needed. "Team Duke" shared insights from employee surveys suggesting that employees felt most valued when they were greeted and acknowledged by others, not just senior management. Employees self-identified as "valued" when people took time to make eye contact, authentically greeted them, and offered positive feedback for their work while moving through or congregating in common areas.

If greetings set the tone, the echoes of laughter register the attitude. We feel humor and congeniality more when there's a sense a workplace is relaxed. The workplace atmosphere should invite comic respite, and it's best if leaders do whatever they can to turn up the volume. I want to be clear: I am encouraging leaders to adopt a practice of injecting humor that includes everyone, is safe and not of a crude nature, and is completely void of any form of social bullying or peer pressure. A culture of cohesion promotes cultural harmony.

The humor should complement the mood and is measured by the amount of hearty laughter, infectious smiles, and nods of congeniality displayed openly in employee gathering areas. People who are relaxed enough to laugh tend to free their minds of unnecessary concerns and stresses to think innovatively. When we feel like we belong, we're able to laugh and enjoy. This is a fast-setting glue to cohesively cement a team, and while I don't have any hard data, I've found that playfulness and being jovial increases productivity.

In the event your organization fails its soundcheck, take a beat. Ask yourself:

1. Are your leaders outwardly recognizing employees for performance?
2. Do you see other employees doing the same to their colleagues?

If you don't see or hear it, employees aren't feeling it. This is a resounding signal your culture lacks cohesion.

Imagine the feeling of value an employee gets when a member of leadership congratulates him for completing an assignment, participating in a community service, finishing an educational achievement, or helping a consumer. Acknowledgment with a handshake, fist bump, or a high five signifies a job well done. These minor efforts can have a major impact on teamwork, performance, and retention. Being able to spot the warnings of a dysfunctional culture and get ahead of the issue positions leaders to act accordingly. These leaders establish that all-elusive mindset that fosters employee retention through actions that create a team atmosphere like offering appreciation when employees perform value-added work. In other words, parts are parts.

## THE FINAL SCENE

Allow me to leave you with this illustration of the talent retention model as if it were a scene from the *Greatest Showman*. From the foundation of people strategies and practices, to the impact of values, beliefs, attitudes and behaviors, the big top is set, and the three rings feature simultaneous performances of belonging, value and commitment. We must look beyond the humorous anecdotal and typical characters portrayed within a circus show—the bearded lady who doesn't know where she belongs, the strongest man in the world who has misplaced his value, and the troubled acrobat who doesn't want to commit—to find the magic of the story.

A simple and catchy beat begins in the background; the spotlight casts a glow upon the set filled with fascinating decorations and colorful characters. We hear the talented and oh-so-handsome (my wife thinks so) Hugh Jackman along with an amazing cast begin to sing: "I come alive." Every character adds a piece to the song, and the music and lyrics build to dramatize what every word means and how it relates to what is happening. By the time it's finished you are standing up, toes tapping, fingers snapping, and you don't want the magic to end. This may be just a tad overdramatic, but I did start college as a theater major, so work with me here.

As the camera pans inside your organization, the CEO and senior leadership speak life to the words, "'Cause you're dreaming with your eyes wide open. And we know we can't go back again." That's exactly how it should be when a Cohesion Culture is in place. You never want to go back to whatever culture you had before. You've tasted it. Not just the kind of taste you get with sugar that is quick to leave. It's the sweet and savory flavor that keeps you wanting more and more.

Each person within the organization has a part to play. These parts bring the culture to life, your greatest show. You hear more of the song and bob your head because you know to "[t]ake the world and redefine it, leave behind your narrow mind. You'll never be the same."

## LESSONS LEARNED

- While leadership is the engine of an organization's failure or success, HR is the fuel that keeps the train on its tracks.
- Talent retention embodies the four elements of emotional and spiritual growth, physical and mental well-being, financial mindset, and intellectual stimuli.
- Learning and relating are a two-pronged approach implemented after the four concepts of the TRM are in place.

----------------

# CHAPTER 6

# There's No Place Like Home

"You've always had the power, my dear.
You just had to learn it for yourself."

**—Glinda (The Good Witch), The Wizard of Oz**

**KEY CONCEPT:**

*1.16*   *Retention:* The rate at which an organization keeps consistent,
long-term employees.

According to the Library of Congress, *The Wizard of Oz* is the most-
watched film of all time. Watching it was a tradition for my family.
Each year, while Dad tinkered in the garage, my brother and I would
cozy up in the living room with our mom to watch this classic. Mom
would take her usual spot on the couch nearest the table with her
reading glasses, Bible, and my grandmother's old lamp. Matt and I
would sit in Aunt Millie's oversized, hand-me-down armchair.

I appreciated that, rather than being a victim of circumstance,
Dorothy put forth her values to guide and direct her actions. It's
something my mom reiterated over and over throughout my childhood.

She'd say, "Being poor is a condition of the pocketbook, not the heart." She insisted that we define others by character, not happenstance.

Years later, when I came to enjoy what I think is the greatest-of-all-time road-trip movie with my children, then my grandchildren, I realized how so many of the characters were leaders in their own right. To me, besides being an epic hero's journey, *The Wizard of Oz* illustrates the sense of belonging that exists when someone experiences what it's like to be part of something extraordinary. I love movies in which the characters work together, strive for a common purpose, and go out of their way to help each other become successful.

Yohana Desta, writing for *Vanity Fair* in November of 2018, reported that a group of Italian researchers from the University of Turin found *The Wizard of Oz* to be "the most influential movie ever." The study was published in *Applied Network Science*. The researchers aimed to measure the success and significance of certain films based on metrics other than box-office success and critical reviews. They focused on subsequent references to these films in other movies, looking through citations available on IMDb. They analyzed 47,000 films from around the world, and *The Wizard of Oz* rose to the top.

I doubt anyone who has seen *The Wizard of Oz* is surprised by this. I certainly wasn't. The sheer, imagistic mastery of the allegorical Yellow Brick Road underpins so many core human values. More than rooting for the underdog, it's also about honesty, decency, servanthood, and compassion. It offers us that rare glimpse into moments of crisis when the what's-in-it-for-me syndrome evaporates as quickly as a dead witch's legs shrivel in the absence of her ruby slippers.

Perhaps first and foremost, *The Wizard of Oz* is a vivid portrait of power and powerlessness. This theme highlights how good people are often powerless, sparking clarity on how many of us associate power with position. At the start, Auntie Em and Uncle Henry are defenseless against mean Miss Gulch, the first adversary—before the tornado, the Wicked Witch, and her apish henchmen. Later on, during the film's defining moment, the audience learns too that the seemingly all-powerful Wizard is also powerless, and that Dorothy possessed the power to find her own way home all along. The only thing missing was the knowledge of how to use it. And she wasn't able to learn that on her own; she needed the other characters in the movie, her team, to make her aware of the power she possessed, just as she did for them.

The real takeaway is that living in a powerless state is self-imposed; character has power to create solutions—and Cohesion Cultures. Regardless of where we find ourselves, each of us has the ability to create a place of unity where values are acknowledged and affirmed. When we create "homes" like this, we're able to commit to personal and organizational success. Indeed, "there is no place like home."

If my career has been anything like Dorothy's adventure, I realize no matter how far I travel or who I am with, when there is value in where I started, then all roads will lead me to a place where I belong. I am a relational guy, and building a Cohesion Culture that works with people who want to be part of it requires a lot of relational underpinning. I have often wholly identified with Dorothy as she clutches her little dog and offers her unforgettable line: "Toto, I've a feeling we're not in Kansas anymore." I too have had to put two and two together to figure things out along the way. I too have thought, "Hey, wait a minute, have we landed somewhere over the rainbow? Where are the people I know and love? What is this strange place? What's with the Technicolor? I thought the world was only black and white."

In creating Cohesion Cultures, organizations take the Yellow Brick Road to find the place they belong: the "somewhere" of quest and commitment. The somewhere that inspires dreams. The somewhere where dreams become visions. Sure, employees might click their heels with the what's-in-it-for-me mindset as they take their first few steps, but like the Tin Man, the Lion, and the Scarecrow, once they have a sense of belonging, they'll see their own value and ultimately commit to something bigger than themselves.

As these characters make their way, attention constantly turns to their personal goals—finding a heart, courage, and brain, as well as helping Dorothy return to Kansas. You might think of this as how leaders first focus on development needs of the employees in tandem with organizational outcomes. Within a culture of cohesion, if Emily claims she wants to someday be the CFO or Thomas in accounting wants to be a trainer, HR strategies and practices provide Emily and Tom with the support they need to reach individual goals. Why? Because effective leaders understand that aligning personal goals to organizational outcomes produces success for everyone.

That's the commitment aspect of cohesion, and that's what the retention model is all about. Leaders align like-minded goals toward future outcomes. Emily will take part in a mentorship program, while Thomas's career will be advanced with an organizational internship— two key activities on the "relating" side of the talent retention model.

## COHESION GENERATES RETENTION

When organizations succeed at cohesion—as they develop individual employees—success is a byproduct. This is how transformation works. For individuals to be engaged in transformative behaviors, they must be willing and capable of focusing on the needs of others before their own.

The charming Scarecrow, forever doubting himself, wanted a brain, the Cowardly Lion sought courage, and the Tin Man a heart. Now, in the case of Dorothy's sidekicks, figuratively speaking, they already had everything they needed, but they needed a leader's affirmational nudge to recognize this. They also genuinely cared for what each other sought and contributed unquestioningly to one another's sense of belonging; just as much as Dorothy cared about getting home, she cared about getting her crew what they cared about too. I'd like to think this was possible in part because they realized they were in the same boat—unable to accomplish their goals on their own. There is a wonderful humility in this that I believe is utterly necessary to the fact that even though they all were eager for their own needs to be met, each of them would have sacrificed their goal if it meant they could help get Dorothy back to Kansas.

Now, just for fun, let's imagine Dorothy is in charge of a multiconglomerate. What are the basic competencies she might need to be an effective leader? Within the context of transforming organizations into cultures of cohesion, today's globalization demands leaders engage and develop five cross-functional competencies. They are:

1.  Develop a level of acumen to ascertain how business, politics, and the environment work.
2.  Explore tastes, trends, and technologies to gain better insight to how ideas will be accepted.
3.  Question why people think as they do, or why things happen as they do.
4.  Adapt to a variety of communications styles that fit others, not just the leader's comfort.
5.  Apply effective problem-solving skills.

Leaders must understand business, politics, and the environment, not only of the country in which they operate but also in the countries where they conduct business. Whether they have an actual facility in those countries or not, their cultures are coming to us as the world flattens more and more, so global leaders need to demonstrate cross-cultural competencies. In other words, it's up to Dorothy to figure out how to navigate within Oz as well as, if not better than, she steered life in Kansas.

Organizational leaders must also learn the tastes, trends, and technologies of other areas. This will avoid ethnocentric thinking, the belief that their own cultural viewpoint is the most important. Instead, they will understand how different cultures came to be and how individuals act in that particular culture, because this shapes the thinking of the individuals in partnership with the leader. Dorothy had to be teachable and learn the nuances of life in Oz.

When presented with new information, leaders must question why—not in an accusatory fashion, but out of a desire to understand. To function effectively as a leader within the Emerald City, Dorothy needed to better understand the sights, sounds, and stories of her surroundings. She found herself confronted with things she knew nothing about or had never seen before. She had to put on her "influence thinking" cap and not take for granted that what she knew about Kansas also applied in Oz.

While Dorothy is being oriented to the great wonders of Oz, there is a horse that changes colors in each subsequent scene. We know the expression today as "a horse of a different color," and it helps to dramatize how the leader's global competencies may be challenged in thinking about where people are from, how they dress, and how they act. Today, when I watch that scene, the horse seems to symbolize the influences that can impact a leader's mind and how the voice of others can play a major role in shaping the actions that leader takes.

Leaders have to adapt to a variety of communication styles, whether it's physical face-to-face interaction, texting on social media platforms, or conducting digital meetings. Technology plays an important role in shaping written, audio, digital, and even nonverbal communication. All of it plays a part in how a leader is perceived and how a leader perceives and influences others.

Think about how much Dorothy and her gang had to figure out on the fly. She didn't get a Facebook alert that warned her of incoming flying monkeys. Waze didn't advise her to avoid the sleep-inducing poppy field. She didn't post "Surrender Dorothy" on Instagram, and no one reposted it on Twitter with the hope of getting a shout-out for backup. Imagine how discombobulating it would be not to have access to outside influences.

Finally, rounding out the five cross-functional competencies for global leaders is problem-solving. Leaders use all the information they acquire about how politics work within regions of the world they must influence; they look at the ways people live and how they incorporate technology in even the simplest of tasks, and what preferred methods and types of communication will be relevant and impactful, and then ask why. Only then can a leader apply tactics to appropriately support the strategic reasoning agreed upon by the leadership of the organization.

I want you to think about what it really means to relate to people on multiple levels from multiple countries with a variety of tastes, trends, and technology. Not everyone you come in contact with in business will be as inviting as the Lollipop Guild, but by the same token, even the Wicked Witch's foot soldiers turned out to be nice guys once the witch was dead.

## THE BETA PHASE

In Chapter 4, I went into detail on what it takes to be a learning organization. Here I want to emphasize that Cohesion Cultures— ones with the best shot at retaining talent—prove themselves time and again when they establish research-and-development budgets and allow for failures.

Teachable leaders accept a certain degree of risk and often describe it as experimentation. Faced with solving a problem, Dorothy put one foot before the other and took her chances on the Yellow Brick Road. What started out as a sure way to a final outcome, her return to Kansas, turned into a series of trials. In facing these, Dorothy made a number of well-calculated decisions along the way. Her one clear misstep was in putting all of her faith into the Wizard of Oz.

A pay-no-attention-to-the-man-behind-the-curtain methodology does not an effective leader make. Leaders need to rely on those who contribute and collaborate. Leaders need to use well-considered data to assess outcomes and predict the potentialities of different footpaths they might follow on the Yellow Brick Road to make headway toward success.

When leaders have a certain freedom to fail without serious consequences of retaliation or retribution, the leader reassesses the "failing" actions and seeks honest feedback. As part of the value system of a learning organization, when an experiment doesn't work, an employee is free to express failure without condemnation. In this fashion the leader promotes a performance-based environment, one that is free from requiring complete perfection to be a success.

If individuals feel they can do no wrong, that's exactly what happens. It is a consequence of human nature. Mistakes will happen. No leader can predict every outcome. Things go sideways, and there are days when no aggregate of good witches has a chance at outnumbering what the bad witches throw your organization's way. Sometimes this means abandoning whatever method you first attempted to find another way of doing something.

For instance, Dorothy thought the Wicked Witch's tyranny would end once Dorothy captured her broom. I suspect that Dorothy would have preferred to convince the witch through good Midwestern charm to give her the broom so she could return home. Of course, the witch had no intention of parting with her broom, or even entering into a civil discussion of lending it to Dorothy for the sake of getting back to the farm.

Little did Dorothy know that to get the broom, she would have to destroy the witch. She had no chance to experiment. She had one shot to get it right. Would this prove too risky for the innocent, sweet farmgirl? This time, Dorothy did not have a house to do her dirty work. Instead, she assessed the resources around her, took a calculated risk, and with the intention of putting out a fire, accidentally melted the witch's wickedness. Which just happened to include the essence of the witch as well. Then, with broom in hand, Dorothy was off to see the Wizard, the wonderful Wizard of Oz.

Throughout the movie, Dorothy succeeded on her own good merits. This does not often work in real life. What Dorothy needed was a mentor—someone who could help her develop her leadership skills. Instead of pointing her westward, it would have been a great idea for the Wizard to give Dorothy a chance to practice what she was learning through an organizational internship.

Dorothy accidentally found cohorts that accepted her and made her feel as though she belonged. She was given responsibility without clear direction of autonomy or initiative. Still she managed to find value in her task to get the broom, and committed wholeheartedly to the task. As we can see in this scenario, Dorothy agreed to bring the broom to the Wizard, the organizational task, because she would be rewarded with her personal goal to return to home.

Unfortunately, and sometimes as it is in real life, the Wizard was less than truthful in his intentions and left her and the gang standing alone while he floated away without providing the help he promised. We see this in organizations when the leader's mindset is not focused on others, but on himself.

At this point, Dorothy had to reevaluate everything she thought was true—that others held all the power to sending her home. And what she found was that even though she'd made mistakes, she'd been learning what she needed to use the power she'd had all along.

## COMMUNICATION STYLES IN REAL LIFE

The talent retention model offers a structure that begins with individuals and the company itself adopting the characteristics of a learning organization and allowing for the transfer of knowledge, specifically about the culture. What tenured employees know about the organization and its nuances is difficult to recap in desk procedures, policies, and other written communication within the organization. Learning organizations sustain their cultures through establishing norms, practicing traditions and rituals, and telling stories. These activities convey the essence of the organization and allow others to learn from the teachers, designers, and good stewards of the culture. This transfer of knowledge occurs through the relational activities of the model.

This process of informal mentoring is known as *acculturation*—an onboarding experience to help new recruits avoid potential cultural landmines. Through these learning experiences, new employees begin to understand what's important to certain leaders and the way those leaders like to receive information, or the way other employees communicate—and even to some degree what various leaders' personalities are like. These nuances, as subtle as they may appear, can speed up the process of feeling connected to others. Knowing about someone else opens the door to more communication and understanding.

Unlike the movie, real life doesn't require a leader to appear in a bubble asking others to "Come out, come out, where ever you are. Come meet the young lady who fell from a star." Leaders do motivate, influence, and enable people of a learning organization to operate like the munchkins and freely share job duties, responsibilities, and offer insight on what it's like in their organization. They just don't need a bubble or a magic wand. These leaders rely on a talent retention model that offers mentorship, organizational internship, and executive coaching to transform learning into relating. Through relational activities, leaders encourage a form of learning that promotes the connection individuals have with those they work with and where they work. This creates value.

Employees (both leaders and followers) should possess a certain level of street-smart savvy to be good social architects and get along with others. For instance, some employees are outgoing in the sense that, personality-wise, they're extroverts. The Tin Man and the Scarecrow were extroverts. These types tend to exhibit trust in others quickly. The Scarecrow immediately took Dorothy by the arm to skip down the path, and the Tin Man trusted Dorothy would find the oil can.

Others are introverted. The beloved munchkins were timid in their initial interactions until they became comfortable. Introverted individuals take longer to establish trust. These types of employees are not found in any one department or unit. Personality profiles that describe how people share ideas, relate to others, convey a sense of urgency, and attend to details offer insight into how others think and act in a variety of situations that will eventually contribute to cohesion and performance.

The Cowardly Lion believed courage was an elusive characteristic bestowed on those who acted with power, even aggression. The lion failed to trust himself first; this contributed to his lack of trust in others. This had been his way of life for so long that it was toughest for him to accept change even though the change was good, even joyful. Once the Cowardly Lion realized his courage came from within, he was freed from the shackles of circumstance and able to claim his victory and, with it, a higher locus of control. Although in the movie this occurred through a self-induced form of self-discovery, in a cohesion-driven organization leaders would have purposefully mentored the lion to bring about this personal discovery of courage.

The way employees prefer to interact with one another doesn't necessarily make them wrong. It's just the way they are, and if you can understand this, then you have a relatively better way to connect with others and foster an environment where all can belong. Connecting the dots between how employees think and act is part of the leadership development activities necessary to retain talent. Opportunities to learn and to put that information to use can easily be offered through mentoring or executive coaching. It's these types of HR practices that make for one of the Best Places to Work, the kind of place that, while it may not be "home" yet, will conjure up the thought, "There's no place like it."

## AUTONOMY AND INITIATIVE

From learning to empowerment, individuals within an organization deserve the freedom to don an entrepreneurial spirit by which autonomy and collaboration work hand in hand to support the growth and development of individual values and commitment. Operating within a prescribed understanding of autonomy creates value for the individual. It signals that the leader trusts and has confidence in the employee's abilities and willingness to perform. This is how the model encourages people to feel valued and have purpose and meaning in what they do.

Autonomy frequently aligns with initiative. Leading others to assert power or initiative maintains an environment of understanding and operating protocol needed for success. Individuals who act first and then tell the supervisor what they've done operate from the highest level of initiative. However, for optimum success, the level of initiative to act first and then inform must be established within the realm of the entrepreneurial spirit, or there could be a disconnect. The Wizard wanted Dorothy to capture the broom and return with it so he could grant her wish to return to her farm, her loved ones, and the comfort of her bed.

The intent of the talent retention model is to ensure that leaders create that perfect Oz, where employees know they belong, have value, and commit to personal and organizational success. Built from the strategies and practices of a well-oiled HR department, the model reflects the organization's culture, and whether it is a Cohesion Culture, through how leaders and employees adopt and exercise their core values, beliefs, attitudes, and behaviors. When leaders fully adopt the model and drive performance and engagement through cohesion, they do more than expect their employees to click their heels three times and dream of home.

And thus, we see how a loose collection of parts becomes a home, because when you give people a reason to belong, they will stay.

## LESSONS LEARNED

- There are key competencies global leaders need to be successful internationally. Beyond knowing their own environment, they must familiarize themselves with what others are doing and why. They must be willing to step out of their own comfort zones and be quick to solve problems.
- Cohesion Culture leaders rely on a talent retention model that offers mentorship, organizational internship, and executive coaching to transform learning into relating.
- Learning organizations sustain their cultures through establishing norms, practicing traditions and rituals, and telling stories.
- These days, more and more employees self-identify as having an entrepreneurial spirit. Smart leaders will embrace such personal initiatives. It's this resourcefulness and ingenuity that drives institutional performance and organizational success.

# *Epilogue*

"You cannot serve the many
until you serve the one."

**–Dr. Troy Hall**

DURING MY CAREER, I HAVE observed that positive change is created when one person steps up, listens to the voices of others, then takes action and makes something happen. Here are two stories that highlight the "power of one" to make positive change in the world.

When it comes to leaders, objectivity, evenhandedness, and letting go of arrogance is the best way to serve others. The leaders below had distinct personalities and distinct ways of doing things. They—along with other successful leaders who have what it takes to master the art of building Cohesion Cultures—also shared specific qualities.

Before leaders focus on the big picture that ultimately allows for many to be served, they must first begin by serving one. We are ill-equipped to make a significant impact in the world if we do not focus on the dignity and respect every single person deserves. It is important to adopt a practice of seeing beyond the many into the one prior to setting tactics in place to foster change for everyone.

## LOUISE HERRING: A PIONEER IN THE CREDIT UNION SPACE

Louise Herring, a pioneer who established over 500 credit unions, understood this. She worked tirelessly to reform the financial services industry to allow folks of modest means to have access to credit and savings services. It might not seem like such a big deal today, but in the 1930s, it meant economic prosperity and the American dream of property ownership and education was possible and equitable for all.

She served as the Ohio delegate to the 1934 national credit union conference, where she signed the original constitution for a national credit union association. To her, credit unions were more than just financial institutions; she believed that credit unions existed to better people's lives. In her own words, "The purpose of the credit union is to reform the financial system, so that everyone can have his place in the sun."

This is how I remember the story: Herring's son, Bill, shared with me that during an effort to organize a credit union at a manufacturing plant, she met an immigrant with a dream. The man wasn't ashamed of his mundane work at the factory, but he had a young son. What this man wanted more than anything was for his son to have a choice. Something that, as an immigrant, he felt he had been denied. Herring understood, and she empathized. It didn't take long before they partnered to make his son's formal education a possibility. Whether or not this kid ultimately had what it took, he deserved options, because everyone deserves the opportunity to improve their financial conditions and educational well-being.

Many years later, late one evening, Herring took ill and was rushed to the hospital. She had been suffering off and on with issues involving damaged heart muscles from long-term health problems. To hear Bill tell it, even in her weakened condition, he never imagined that his mother—with her lioness heart, her responsive integrity, and her razor-sharp sense of service—wouldn't make it through surgery, and yet the cards weren't at all in her favor.

As Bill recalled, it was a long night. When he entered her room the next morning, he saw a young man, a surgeon to be exact, holding his mother's hand. After introductions, it became clear to Bill that this man, the one who operated on his mother, was the son of the immigrant worker she had helped to start an education fund. Louise did not help the factory worker so that one day she might benefit. She helped him because she was committed to all people having a better life—one that offered people a place to belong and to have value through financial freedoms and education. A life committed to helping others, not for the sake of personal gain, but because it was the right thing to do.

## KENYA: TWO MEN AND A SEWING MACHINE

In 2017, I served on a global team working with business, government, and community leaders in Kenya to extend the teachings of savings mobilization and credit utilization throughout Africa. While on a field engagement, I met two men. They were young, in their early twenties at best, and hailed from a township that was notoriously corrupt, where citizens feared for their lives, and drug use and prostitution was rampant. A neighboring village elder had given these residents a chance at a better life. Arguably, these men could have high-tailed it to a bigger, better place, one that held promise and better opportunities, and yet, these prodigal men decided to return home and make a difference.

When I asked why, they said they wanted to change the way people treated each other and that they had a plan. The goal was to set up a business where at-risk women could learn a trade. They would teach these women how to sew. It was extremely important to give these women an opportunity to express self-worth and earn money from a business that did not require them to sell their dignity for dollars.

Realizing that endeavors of this sort in the United States usually involve a wide-scale program, I asked them how many sewing machines they had. In unison, they responded, "One." I tried to process this and immediately began to apply American standards. My follow-up inquiry met with a similar response. They had one woman interested.

I began to experience the problem that occurs when leaders impose their cultural views and understanding upon others. While I was looking for a way to impact the lives of many, my perspective changed to understand the importance of serving the one before the many.

They went on to explain that if they could get just one woman to fully make the transition, then others would see sewing as a sustainable career option. These men knew that with change comes skepticism, and only proof can meet the demands of doubt and change the mind. They further surmised that she would become an advocate, and, eventually, one would become two, then four, and so on and so on. These young leaders didn't see at-risk women in their village as broken, but as beacons of hope who had the power, even the audacity, to change their lives and be change-agents in the lives of others.

Once we take an idea, give it shape, and share it, we begin influencing others. In this case, I have every confidence that the woman who works with them will feel as if she belongs and that she has value, and that she will make a commitment to the effort and add to the community's newly found identity. If for no other reason than these young entrepreneurs' enthusiastic, altogether altruistic approach, it's clear to me they will effect great, big, beautiful life-affirming changes in their communities and that, however inherently or intuitively they arrived at it, they were well on their way to mastering Cohesion Culture and talent retention.

# *Acknowledgments*

I HAVE ALWAYS CONSIDERED MYSELF a work in progress, understanding from my faith that God is not done with me yet.

But He has not been in this task alone. My dad and mom played significant roles in my development. Dad, the protector and provider, and Mom, the nurturer and caregiver, provided me with many opportunities to learn and self-discover. In fact, my mom was instrumental in teaching me how to think about life, listen to the respected voices of those I could trust and put forth actions that were honest and honorable.

Vickie, my high school sweetheart and wife, has supported and loved me for more than forty-five years. She has contributed much "wife wisdom" and keeps me from getting too far ahead of myself.

My strongest allies and colleagues at work, Scott Woods and Leslie Norris, give me space to be creative and pour into me in the way only true friends can take a seed and make it a tree. I am grateful to work with a board of directors that supports a people-centric philosophy where employees are wanted and needed, valued for what they do, and supported to achieve personal and organizational success.

My heart is full to be surrounded by so many loving and caring people. My cup truly runneth over.

CPSIA information can be obtained
at www.ICGtesting.com
Printed in the USA
LVHW110009221019
634942LV00006B/863/P